EMERGENC

Delta Books of Interest

EMERGENCE

THE REBIRTH OF THE SACRED

David Spangler

A DELTA/MERLOYD LAWRENCE BOOK

A Delta/Merloyd Lawrence Book
Published by
Dell Publishing
a division of
Bantam Doubleday Dell Publishing Group, Inc.
666 Fifth Avenue
New York, New York 10103

Printed in the United States of America

Published simultaneously in Canada

One previous Delta edition

New Delta edition—November 1989

10 9 8 7 6 5 4 3 2 1

BG

Library of Congress Cataloging in Publication Data

Spangler, David
   Emergence: the rebirth of the sacred.

   "A Merloyd Lawrence book."
   1. Religious sciences.   2. Spangler, David.
I. Title.
BF1999.S6188   1984   001.9
ISBN: 0-385-29311-9
Library of Congress Catalog Card Number 83-7626

To my two families:
Julie, John-Michael, Myrtle, Marshall, and Hazel
and
the LORIANS
and in special loving memory to
MAY HANNA,
who never lost faith in emergence.

Contents

Introduction

David Spangler is a highly regarded advocate of spiritual empowerment, a recognized influence in the so-called "new age" movement. He partakes of the same "grounded transcendence" that he ascribes to the Cathedral of St. John the Divine (p. 23), for he is both "down-to-earth" and a genuine mystic.

His deepest concern is the empowerment of people to be truly liberated, true participants in the "new age." This concern arises from his awareness of the way in which the world has changed in recent years and, more importantly, of the major paradigm shift in his own thinking. For twenty-five years this has also been my own primary intellectual interest, and the discovery that David and I shared this has been a key element of our friendship.

The world has changed drastically in a very short time. In past ages people tended to live and die in the same small communities in which they were born. In this context, ethnicity and traditions could persist. But this has not been true for some time and certainly is not true now. Radical cultural transformation has become the password of our civilization.

Such generalizations will seem simplistic to many readers, but to me they are almost daily made agonizingly clear. For my work is in one of the most traditional of institutions, a religious institution, and very often I am dealing with persons who resist or refuse to accept the fact of change. They are, by and large, persons who can understand faith only in terms of images and constructs that flowered in an earlier age. They tend to become fundamentalists, holding on to the *forms* of another period. Ignoring St. Paul's warning that the treasure is in earthen vessels, they tend to absolutize the vessels.

Many others have gone in quest of a new world view as they sensed that the old patterns were not holding. David gives a description, as well as a most valuable critique, of some of the early "new age" groups with which he had first-hand experience. The hallmark of these groups—those waiting for a Technicolor apocalypse, UFO-borne messiahs, or a cataclysmic natural disaster to usher in the "new age"—is a sense of powerlessness. David's mind-set is very different, thus demonstrating that not all "new age" thought is cast in the same mold.

David shows that the paradigm of the "new age" is really "the planetary village," the image of the interdependency of all things. Rene Dubos used the term "symbiosis" for this phenomenon in his work as a microbiologist concerned with the delicate balance of all life. The new physics recognizes that matter and energy, which we used to think of as particles, are also pulsations—one movement moving into another—so that, in Gregory Bateson's term, the pattern that connects becomes the only "constant." When you examine these patterns, you are not looking for fixed objects, for all is in flux. But within the flux are eddies of predictable patterns.

These new discoveries about the reality of nature, of all matter, are similar to recent insights by such theologians and philosophers as Lewis Mumford, Thomas Berry, Pierre de Chardin, William I. Thompson, and Fred Polak, among others. David draws from their thought as he develops his own constructs for empowerment.

For me, David's thought closely parallels the essence of Christian tradition, particularly as I find it in the writings of Alexander Schmemann, a contemporary Russian Orthodox theologian and F. D. Maurice, a nineteenth-century Anglican theologian whose views were denounced as "universalist" by his contemporaries but whose thought has won new appreciation in recent years, thanks to the former Archbishop of Canterbury, Michael Ramsey.

For both Schmemann and Maurice the Church explains
itself in categories of the Kingdom, in categories of time
rather than place, and ecclesiology is necessarily sacramental (eucharistic), centering around Paul's perception
that in the fullness of the Kingdom (which we now experience *in sacramento*) "Christ is all in all" (Col. 3:11). *Christ
himself becomes the pattern which connects all things.*

Thus, when David speaks of "the resacralization" of the
world, he points to a spiritual reality that is already manifest materially. He gives us some philosophical categories
that allow one to be an orthodox, incarnational Christian
and at the same time become a "universalist" (a "catho-
lic"), recognizing one's fellowship (one's communion) in
the sisterhood and brotherhood of all creation.

This brings up the fascinating question of the relationship of this vision with other religious traditions—and the
beginnings of an answer are apparent. If we are all part of
"the earth community," if the human presence is part of, is
never separate from, the rest of the earth—is indeed precisely the consciousness of the earth—then we are very
much part of the "Christ is all in all" pattern. Just as the
eucharistic bread becomes Christ in the "time" of the Kingdom, so too Christ in the time of the Kingdom also becomes
every other part of creation. Thus one moves into a highly
sacramental and splendid doctrine of Creation in which the
presence of God is visible in nature, because in the Kingdom all nature is transparent to Christ.

The recovery of this Kingdom dimension of Christian
doctrine is assisted in some measure by our intercourse in
recent years with Far Eastern mystical thought, which has
always been "heavy" with nature. Modern ecological understanding also becomes inevitable and generic Christian
givens because they are incarnational and sacramental.

The problem I find in much Christian thought and practice is the tendency to create separations, exclusions—
whereas, following the theology of Schmemann, Maurice,

and Spangler, NOTHING can be "left out." The Church cannot ever be big enough—because the Kingdom Church is the "flip side" of creation; baptism represents a joining with, not an exclusion from. Communion indeed is *union with all*, as Christ is all in all.

Consciously or subconsciously, virtually everyone in western civilization, at least, has been forced to shift mental gears in the last thirty years. David's account of his "journeys" will encourage many to explore their own internal pathways, even as he invites them into the emerging "planetary village" of the Kingdom.

James Parks Morton
Dean of the Cathedral of St. John the Divine
New York City
June 1983

PART I The Dream

Now I a fourfold vision see
And a fourfold vision is given to me;
'Tis fourfold in my supreme delight
And threefold in soft Beulah's night
And twofold always. May God keep us
From Single vision & Newton's sleep!

—WILLIAM BLAKE

1

New Vision

WILLIAM SPANGLER, MY PATERNAL GRANDFATHER, DIED BE-
fore I was born, but I came to know him through stories
my father would tell. Ohio farmer, engineer, state senator,
inventor (he held several patents on improvements to the
cash register), he lived a rich and productive life, generally
concerning himself with very down-to-earth projects.

Apparently, though, Granddad's mind had some pull to
the stars, too, for he was an early investigator of rocketry.
He had a small laboratory and workshop on the farm, and
there he would initiate my father, Marshall, into the mysteries of aerodynamics, chemical propulsion, and space
travel. He would assemble a rocket, then the two of them
would go out into a field to launch it. Once, in a burst of
experimental enthusiasm, my father caught a field mouse

and put it in the nose cone of one of their prototypes. Once launched, the craft and its passenger disappeared from sight, neither to be seen again.

My grandfather's interest in rockets did not extend to stories about them. My father, however, would save his nickels and pennies and buy copies of *Amazing Science Fiction Stories* and other pulp science fiction magazines, which he would read late at night under the covers of his bed with a flashlight. Subterfuge was necessary, since Granddad considered such magazines as trash and would burn them in the big kitchen wood stove whenever he found them.

After my father had grown up, becoming a scientist himself, specializing in the relationship of engineering and the biological sciences, he continued his love of science fiction, building a fairly extensive collection of books and magazines. This used to be one of my favorite sections in our large library at home. We would have long discussions about the ideas contained in many of these books, often while sitting outside at night looking at the stars through a telescope he and my mother, Hazel, had given me. What possibilities existed in the universe beyond the earth? What life, what cultures, what knowledge and perspectives might await us Out There? More importantly, what might we learn to see more clearly about ourselves and our own world if we could see them from a more universal perspective?

These memories of our family love affair with exploration, space, and a planetary perspective came back to me with special clarity one day in 1974. A brilliant scholar and friend of mine, William Irwin Thompson, had created a new educational organization called the Lindisfarne Association, housing it in an old resort inn in eastern Long Island. There he was holding the first conference of an affiliated association of scholars, visionaries, and activists in many fields, called the Lindisfarne Fellows, all of whom shared with Bill and myself an interest in the emergence of a new planetary culture.

It was a rich collection of minds and insights, including such persons as Richard Baker, roshi (or abbot) of the Zen Center in San Francisco; Gregory Bateson, anthropologist and cyberneticist; the sociologist Elise Boulding; Stewart Brand, publisher of the *Whole Earth Catalog* and *Co-Evolution Quarterly*; Saul Mendlovitz of the Institute for World Order; economist Fritz Schumacher, the author of the groundbreaking work *Small Is Beautiful*; Paolo Soleri, architect and founder of Arcosanti in Arizona; the Benedictine ecumenical scholar and monk, Brother David Steindl-Rast; and Nancy and John Todd, biologists, ecologists, artists, and founders of the New Alchemy Institute.

The conference was set up to allow each speaker both to give his or her own presentation and to add commentary to that of another. To my delight, I discovered that as a commentator, I had been paired with *Apollo* 9 astronaut Russell Schweickart. From a distance, Rusty looks like a nineteen-year-old, his red hair in perfect accord with his nickname. When he was first pointed out to me, I was shocked. Slim and vibrant, he seemed more like a boyish adventurer straight out of my childhood fantasies of Tom Swift and his cosmic escapades than one of the NASA astronauts.

Of all the presentations given at that conference, and there were many fine ones, Rusty's stands out for me. He spoke in the second person, telling the story of his flight as the first lunar module pilot in earth orbit in March 1969. Such was his eloquence as a storyteller that it seemed as if each of us was in that ship with him. The text of his talk is reprinted in *Earth's Answer*, a Lindisfarne book published in 1977 by Harper and Row, from which I share the following quote:

[Talking about looking down upon the earth from orbit] And you identify with Houston and then you identify with Los Angeles and Phoenix and New Orleans. And the next thing you recognize in yourself is that you're identifying with North Africa—you look forward to that, you anticipate it, and there it is. And that whole process of what it is you identify with begins to shift. When you go around the Earth in an hour and a half, you begin to recognize that your identity is with that whole thing. And that makes a change.

Sitting next to Rusty as he magically wove his tale, I experienced a shift of perspective so sudden and distinct that I thought I could hear a snap inside me. In that moment, I was in memory back with my father, reliving his stories of Granddad and the rockets, reexperiencing our discussions of science fiction stories and our speculations of what it would be like when human beings actually went into space. Along with that memory came a realization, a change in my sense of reality. For here, sitting beside me in the flesh, was a real-life, honest-to-goodness spaceman, no longer a creature of imagination or fiction but someone who had actually been Out There!

I suddenly realized that I was living in a world that had been a dream of my grandfather and my father, a world in which we had transcended old boundaries to gain a new vision. No longer a dream of writers, now it was our world, the real world. Because this was so, like Rusty, we, too, as humanity, could now see ourselves from Out There, with all the possibilities for change and new identity which such a vision implies. Beyond speculations and philosophies, we could now begin to see another earth than the one revealed only through our earthbound perspectives. We could see the earth in its wholeness, and ourselves as part of that wholeness.

At the end of his talk, Rusty commented on this issue of perspective and new vision:

You know very well . . . you're the sensing element for man. You look down and see the surface of that globe that you've lived on all this time and you know all those people down there and they are like you, they are you— and somehow you represent them. You are up there as the sensing element. . . . The eye that doesn't see doesn't do justice to the body. That's why it's there; that's why you are out there.

My grandfather was such a "sensing element." Working in his laboratory or standing on the slopes of an Ohio hill, watching a makeshift rocket climb the heavens, he was looking ahead, striving for the vision of a new world. The same is true for my father, who, though never having been in orbit, still has always seen the world in its wholeness. The same is true for each of us. We are the eyes to see our world, the sensing elements to see ourselves. In us, whoever or wherever we are, lie the possibilities for new vision. To explore those possibilities, to be open to the seeing that promotes unfoldment is to do justice to our world. That's why we're here.

2

Rebirth of the Sacred

IN THE TWENTY-NINTH CHAPTER OF PROVERBS WE FIND THE familiar statement "Where there is no vision, the people perish." A vision means hope. It means a guiding direction. It can also mean something else: inspiration for a people to transcend themselves, to transform, to strive not just to be better but also to be different.

That is the quality which a Dutchman, Fred Polak, describes in *The Image of the Future*. He points out the importance of a vision of the future to the development and vitality of any civilization. Using various examples from history, he demonstrates that without a vision of the future, a culture loses its creative power and begins to stagnate, eventually to die. However, this vision is not just an image of what might happen tomorrow. Polak terms it the image of "The Other," by which he means that which is unknown and potentially transformative. Implicit within it is an acceptance of forces in the universe which humanity cannot ultimately control or predict.

These forces, existing in the mystery of God or in the depths of humankind, render the future itself mysterious and unpredictable to some degree. As part of an image of the future, people must accept and embrace the mystery of tomorrow without insecurity. Such a vision challenges the culture to dare, to be open to change, and to accept a spirit of creativity that could alter its very structure. A willingness to explore helps a civilization avoid complacency and stimulates vitality.

The message behind Polak's book was that western civilization was losing or even had lost its image of the future and was therefore in the beginning stages of stagnation and decay. Considering the fascination that our culture has with the future, this may seem a faulty diagnosis. However, *The Image of the Future* was written nearly thirty years ago, before much of the current interest and work in future studies began. (Indeed, Polak was one of those who initiated such studies as an academic discipline and was one of the first to call himself a futurist.)

Polak himself clarifies this point by distinguishing between an image of the future and a linear image of progress. The former has a transformational component, while the latter does not. Instead, progress (as our culture generally thinks of it) is only an image of the present projected into the future. While it anticipates differences, they are more surface changes than real transformations.

I am reminded of the television series *Star Trek*, which postulates a star-spanning civilization several hundred years in the future. Though the scenery and tools are different and several species of aliens abound, the humans and the Federation for which they work would be instantly recognizable to any modern American. Little transformation of culture is evident in the form of new motivations, new social organizations, new kinds of values, or new modes of consciousness. Of course, as a show broadcast over a popular medium, its theme is not transformation but adventure, and thus the characters must not be so different that a viewer of today could not identify with them. Still, is it reasonable to assume that after hundreds of years of progress, space travel, contact with alien races and cultures, and so forth, the Federation would be nothing more than twentieth-century North American culture transplanted?

When we think of progress, however, it is often just this kind of transplantation of the present into the future that we have in mind. Our minds, expectations, and imaginations become prisoners of what we already know, captives of the familiar. Transformation can be a frightening notion; to avoid it, we can hide behind a safer image of linear progress in which change seems predictable and controllable. The more things change, the more they stay the same.

Progress need not be seen in this way. Robert Nisbet, in his *History of the Idea of Progress*, writes that throughout western history, the idea of progress has been organically intertwined with an image of the sacred. It has traditionally included some element of the encounter with a transcendental Other, such as the will of God or the sense of a divine purpose operating within history. This element is the same awareness that empowers Polak's image of the future.

In the latter two-thirds of the twentieth century, however, as both authors point out, the idea of the sacred and of the Other as an influential part of human destiny has largely been deleted from the intellectual climate. The result has been the flattening out of our concept of progress, draining it of its transcendental and transformative power, until it has become simply a reflection of what we already know.

I grew up with an affinity for the future. Given my family background, this is not surprising. Science, technological progress, and the idea of human destiny were everyday themes in our household. My childhood heroes were explorers, particularly in the fields of science, men and women who furthered human knowledge and experience. I was a devoted fan of Tom Swift, Jr., a fictional young scientist, and my fantasies were invariably of journeying into space and adventuring on strange, distant worlds.

Yet it was not just progress that we celebrated in our family. Though a scientist and engineer himself, my father's deepest interest was in people, which was equally true for my mother. They were fascinated by creativity, by the manner in which people made changes and affected history. Consequently, their interest in the future was really a fascination with how the idea of the future stimulated the imaginative, creative act.

This attitude supported another theme in my own life. From a very early age, I was aware of an extra dimension or presence to the world around me, which as I grew older I came to identify as a sacred or transcendental dimension. I don't remember discussing this awareness very much; it seemed so natural that I don't think it really occurred to me to talk about it. However, everything about my parents' lives and actions implicitly affirmed this awareness, in particular their attitudes toward the creative potentials of human beings and our inner powers of spirit to mobilize those potentials through vision and inspiration. They were givers of hope. From them I learned that an image of the future that does not inspire hope does not liberate our inner energies to struggle and build for a worthy tomorrow.

In my work I travel extensively and lecture; my theme is usually spirituality and our connection with the sacred dimension of our lives, but I also speak frequently about the future. Wherever I have gone in North America, I have found a common theme in questions that audiences ask. Is there hope? Do we really have a future? In the minds of many, progress is now synonymous with technological advancement, which has brought us to the brink of nuclear holocaust. As such, it offers us no transformational options. It gives no suggestion as to how we can make a difference. Without a sense that there is a force of creativity and imagination—whether within ourselves or within the sacredness of the universe—that can go beyond the habits and expectations of the present, how can an image of the future survive beneath the fearful shadow of The Bomb?

We live in a time, as Polak foresaw, when the idea of the future is threatened with extinction, whether from fear or from the loss of a sense of the sacred, of a transformational expectation. If the future dies within us, we are disempowered. We lose the sense that we can shape our history, that, in fact, choice is even possible. We lose our will to change.

Fortunately, the future is not down and out, not yet. Since Polak wrote his book thirty years ago, a transformational impulse has appeared. Appearing in different guises and called by different names, it represents a resurgence of hope, of vision, and of creative activity on behalf of a better civilization. At its heart, it is a rebirth of our sense of the sacred. By this I mean, however, not just a sense of something transcendent and otherworldly; I mean as well a recognition of the value and sacredness in ourselves—in our humanness—and also in the natural world about us, and in our destiny.

This impulse has been the context for my work for the past twenty years. It offers an empowering vision, a setting for creativity, a direction for choice. It is a chance to imagine and fashion a culture in which we may not only survive but do justice to our humanity and the potentials inherent within us. I call it the image of a new age, the vision of emergence.

3

The Old Idea of a New Age

So we stand on the brink of a new age: the age of an open world and of a self capable of playing its part in that larger sphere. An age of renewal, when work and leisure and learning and love will unite to produce a fresh form for every stage of life, and a higher trajectory for life as a whole.

THE HISTORIAN LEWIS MUMFORD WROTE THESE WORDS IN 1956 in *The Transformations of Man*. In that work he traced the development of human culture through five great transformations, concluding with his vision that humanity now stands on the brink of another global change, perhaps the most significant one yet.

I was eleven years old and living in Morocco when Mumford published this book. At the time, ideas of cultural transformation or the beginning of a new age were far from my mind. We had been in Morocco since 1951 when my father, who was working for the United States government, had been assigned there, and the excitement of growing up in this most exotic of lands—indeed, just the excitement of growing up, period—was more than enough to occupy my attention.

A year later, in 1957, we returned to North America, settling in Old Deerfield, a colonial village in the Berkshires of western Massachusetts. There I attended Deerfield Academy, a prep school for boys, a large cultural leap from my life in Morocco. Needless to say, in adjusting to this new environment my thoughts were still far away from images of the future. It was challenging enough coping with the present! However, in 1959 we moved again, this time to Phoenix, Arizona, and for me this was more than just a move to another place. In Phoenix I encountered a new vision of life.

While we were still in Morocco, my parents, along with numerous other people living on the air base where we were, had had a sighting of a UFO. This object, which had been tracked by radar as it traveled at unbelievable speed from the North Atlantic, across Spain, over Morocco, and south into equatorial Africa before it finally disappeared, was not the traditional saucer shape. As my mother described it to me, it was more like a great cigar, a cylinder pointed at one end, covered with coruscating lights, leaving what appeared to be a trail of fire behind it. So memorable was this sight that it inaugurated an interest in our family in the phenomenon of unidentified flying objects.

Phoenix in the late fifties was still something of a frontier city, just beginning to grow with the arrival of new electronic industries and housing developments. It was a mecca for those with health problems, particularly of a respiratory nature (which included me, as I was then suffering from asthma), as well as for those who simply enjoyed the beauty and open spaces of the surrounding desert. It was also the home of several groups exploring the UFO phenomenon, since these open spaces and the clear desert air at night made ideal conditions for attempting sightings.

Following up on our family interest, we made contact with some of these groups and joined one, only to discover that UFO's were not the only thing on their minds. Most of our new friends also proved to be interested in and actively exploring parapsychological phenomena as well, such as ESP and the deeper powers of the human mind and soul. Another thread that linked many of these groups to each other, and to similar groups in other parts of the country, was a belief in the imminent dawning of a new age.

As I encountered it then, this belief was fairly straightforward. The earth was entering a new cycle of evolution, which would be marked by the appearance of a new consciousness within humanity that would give birth to a new civilization. Unfortunately, the present cultures of the world were so corrupt and locked into materialism that they would resist this change. Consequently, the transition from one age to another would be accomplished by the destruction of the old civilization, either by natural causes such as earthquakes and floods, or by a great world war, or by social collapse of an economic and political nature, or by combinations of these. However, those individuals whose consciousness could become attuned to and one with the qualities of the new culture would be protected in various ways and would survive the time of cataclysms and disasters. They would then enter a new age of abundance and spiritual enlightenment—the Age of Aquarius, as astrologers call it—in which, guided by advanced beings, perhaps angels or spiritual masters or perhaps emissaries from an

extraterrestrial civilization whose spacecraft were the
UFO's, they would help to create a new civilization.

This belief took various forms. For some the idea was
distinctly tied up with the belief in UFO's, for others it was
religious in tone, and for still others it was economic and
revolutionary. Some groups arrived at the belief through
some form of revelation or prophecy; others did so through
historical analysis and a considered examination of modern
cultural trends. The essential idea, however—that our civilization is in the midst of a significant transformation which
would produce, in Mumford's words, "a higher trajectory
for life as a whole"—was the connecting link. It was the
core around which an international subculture of expectation and anticipation had formed.

Where did this idea come from? How could people believe in it? In the form in which I first encountered it, the
image of a new age had several parents. As the term *Age
of Aquarius* suggests, one source was astrology and its
teaching that evolution goes through cycles, corresponding
to the signs of the zodiac, and each approximately 2000 to
2400 years in length. We are now moving from the cycle
associated with Pisces into the one associated with
Aquarius. Another source is the idea of evolution itself
translated from the physical realm into the sphere of psy-
chological and spiritual development on the scale of the
whole of humanity. In this context, civilizations, like individuals, go through profound changes from time to time
which represent discontinuities; that is, a jump or shift is
made from one evolutionary condition to another. The new
age is such a shift.

The idea of the new age as a spiritual phenomenon
comes from mystical and psychic revelations and the pre-
dictions of prophets such as Nostradamus and, more recently, the American psychic Edgar Cayce. It is also
discussed and prophesied in the work of metaphysical and
esoteric groups such as the Theosophical Society and the

Lucis Trust, which publishes the writings and teachings of Alice Bailey. Another source is anthroposophy, a spiritual doctrine that grew out of the teachings of the Austrian mystic and scientist Rudolf Steiner. While Steiner's writings do not discuss the idea of a new age as explicitly as some of the other sources mentioned, in his innovative integration of spiritual perception and insights with such fields as education, agriculture, medicine, the care of the retarded, and practical politics he prefigured many of the attitudes and techniques that a new age culture might embody.

There are also prophecies found in the spiritual traditions of other cultures. For example, there is a Central American prophecy, connected with the Mayan and Aztec civilizations, that a cycle of "dark ages" will come to an end in 1987 with a time of great cleansing, the severity of which will depend on the choices and attunement of humanity; following this, a new age of harmony and wholeness will emerge. The Hopi Indians of the American Southwest have a similar prophecy, also focused on the period from 1980 to 2000 A.D. as a time of transition into a new cycle of cooperation.

Thus, the image of a new age is not really new at all. Its echoes can be found in many cultures throughout history. However, its roots go especially deep into western cultural and religious tradition, stemming ultimately from the whole Judeo-Christian belief in a coming, in the advent of a new and sacred spirit upon the earth. Whether this spirit is seen as Christ in a second coming or as another messiah, the anticipation of a millennium and of a utopian civilization has been one of the driving forces in the history of western development. In fact, in some of its expressions, the idea of the new age (certainly as I first encountered it) is identical in spirit if not always in language to many of the current millennial expectations of evangelical and fundamentalist

Christian groups. One need only read the publications of organizations such as the Seventh-Day Adventists to find such similarities as the imminent end of history as we know it, with the destruction of the nations but with the survival into a new age of an elect.

As to why so many people have accepted this idea so strongly in these days, there are undoubtedly many reasons. Certainly, the stresses and tensions of our time, the threat of nuclear holocaust, the pace of technological change, the seeming disintegration of traditional modes of behavior, all lend power to an apocalyptic climate. The end of the century and of the millennium is near, traditionally a time when millennial movements appear. Also, for those who are sensitive to such things, there are all the prophecies that I have mentioned and many more besides that point to this time as being a transformative threshold for humanity (and these prophecies do not have to be psychic in nature, unless you classify Mumford as such!).

However, I feel there are reasons that cannot be pointed to logically, reasons of intuition and spirit. When I first encountered in Phoenix the image of the Aquarian Age, the new age, something deep inside me said yes to it. Those depths continue to say yes twenty-four years later, even though throughout those intervening years I have struggled with the ways in which that image is often given expression and have sought a clearer reality behind the many varied expectations that it inspires.

As Polak has said, our culture does not always offer us an image of the future that inspires us to efforts of transformation. We hunger for that image, which is not a hunger for a vision of tomorrow but for a vision of ourselves. We look for what will proclaim us as beings of choice and development and empower our capacities for growth. All too often what we find in its place is the disempowerment of hopelessness and habit and the vitiated vision of those who can only see the future as the reflection of the present. It is no wonder, then, that the idea of a new age, properly understood and expressed as a transformative image of the future, should find a welcome in our midst.

4

From UFO's to Findhorn:
Journeys Along the Brink

IN AUGUST 1964, WHEN I WAS NINETEEN AND LIVING IN
Phoenix, I gave my first public lecture on the new age. It
was at a conference attended by people from various spiritual groups around the United States who already had a
commitment to that idea. As such they constituted a unique
audience whose interest in a prophetic vision of personal
and global transformation was not generally shared or understood by the average American of that time. Eighteen
years later, in December 1982, I gave the first of four Advent sermons at the Cathedral of St. John the Divine, in
New York City, on the theme of spirituality and the new
age. This time, by contrast with my first public talk, the audience was not a select and private gathering of believers
sharing an esoteric prophetic vision. Rather, it was a cross

section of ordinary Americans living in a time when the
ideas of transformation and a new age had become familiar
and acceptable enough to be discussed in an institution as
mainstream and public as the cathedral.

In between these two events there had been for me
eighteen years of journeying along "the brink of a new age,"
as Mumford put it. From California to Great Britain, from
Canada to Florida, I have worked with individuals and
groups who have gathered on that brink with me, all interested in discovering and implementing a new and positive
image of the future. During that time I have observed the
idea of a new age widen from being the experience of a
brink into something more like a plateau on which to stand,
a foundation which could support serious creative action on
behalf of a new world.

Though I initially encountered the idea of a new age in
1959, my first steps along the brink did not really come
until the spring of 1965, almost a year after my first public
talk. During the intervening months I had been receiving
other lecture invitations. (Appropriately, these invitations
came mostly from California, the mecca of apocalyptic visions, where even in those days people were expecting to
inaugurate the new age with a statewide plunge into the
Pacific.) At the same time, I had been resolving an inner
conflict. I was then happily engaged in college, working for
a degree in genetics. At the same time, I was experiencing
something akin to a religious call, as an inner part of me
that had earlier said yes to the idea of a new age now
sought to explore and serve the emergence of that idea in
whatever way it could.

Because of a background of psychic and mystical experiences during childhood that had left me with a deep interest in the nature of spirituality and the role of the invisible, formative side of life, that inner call won out.
Accordingly, I left college and headed for Los Angeles.

There I was joined by a friend of our family, Myrtle Glines, who has been my partner and colleague ever since.

Myrtle is a highly intuitive and skilled human relations counselor, with a profound ability to place people in touch with their inner, spiritual potentials. She had raised a family of four children, the youngest of whom had recently been married, and had built up a successful counselor training school in Salt Lake City, Utah. At the time we began working together, she was making a transition in her own life, embarking on a spiritual quest and following her own growing interest in the image of a new age.

We discovered we complemented each other very well, as each had experience with one half of the human wholeness. To our work together, Myrtle brought her insights and wisdom concerning the personality, while I added my experiences with the spiritual nature of life. We were each other's teachers, and as we developed a lecturing and counseling service together we were able to offer a more holistic perspective to others. Also, in those days, when I looked a good five years younger than I was and was still discovering how best to express the things I wished to share, it didn't hurt to have a wise white-haired woman thirty-seven years my senior as a partner. With her practical insights into human problems and their resolution, Myrtle definitely gave me and my mystical musings credibility.

In 1970 William Irwin Thompson wrote, in a book aptly called *At the Edge of History*, that it would "seem that we are at one of those moments when the whole meaning of nature, self, and civilization is overturned in a re-visioning of history as important as any technological innovation." Similarly, two years later, a former senior editor of *Look* magazine, George Leonard, wrote *The Transformation*, in which he said that "the current period is indeed unique in history" and that "it represents the beginning of the most thoroughgoing change in the quality of human existence since . . . the birth of civilized states some five thousand years ago."

This is a powerful and comprehensive vision. When Myrtle and I began working together in 1965, however, there weren't many places where such a vision was being taken seriously or even considered, at least not in traditional educational, political, or religious circles. To find it, even in a narrow form, and to work with it required entering what I called the "new age subculture." This was a very loosely associated circuit of groups and organizations scattered throughout the United States but mostly concentrated along the two coasts and in the Southwest.

Most of these were informal study groups, people gathered to read and explore the writings of visionaries and metaphysical prophets such as Edgar Cayce, Joel Goldsmith, Alice Bailey, and Rudolf Steiner, or to sponsor studies into ESP, UFO's, the psychology of mystical states, or altered states of consciousness. Others were churches or organizations such as Unity, Science of Mind, Spiritualists, Theosophists, Sufis, and Rosicrucians. Still others were formed around no particular teacher or with no discernible philosophy but simply to "study" or talk about or promote the "New Age." Some of these latter would form around a particular prophecy, becoming very active and proselytizing as the designated date approached for the new age to begin (as evidenced by some spectacular planetwide event), and then usually disbanding when that particular event failed to materialize.

Myrtle and I entered this world not unlike babes entering a forest. Within it we found, as one might expect, people and groups who were deluded (or the deluders), unbalanced emotionally, disconnected from reality, and at times downright weird. These were the exceptions, however, and we learned to recognize them and avoid them. For the most part we met kindhearted, sincere people, many of them with remarkable powers of intuition and inner vision, all moved by the idea of participating in some way in the emergence of a new and healthier world. Indeed, since the focus of Myrtle's and my work was on developing inner and outer balance, good human relations, and a healthy integration of the personality and the spirit, we tended not to attract to ourselves the "crazies" or those who simply sought escape into otherworldly fantasies. (Though I am sure that there were those who felt that our spiritual emphasis and our commitment to a vision of a new age marked us as two of the "crazies" ourselves!)

What we quickly discovered in our work, though, was the shadow side of the new age movement. Glamour, imbalance, withdrawal from society, and a false sense of righteous (and separative) superiority were some of its manifestations. There were others, and I will discuss them later. However, for both of us, the most immediate failing of this vision was that in spite of its promise of a new world, it was ultimately disempowering. It was not, in Polak's terms, a true image of the future.

As I pointed out in the previous chapter, the idea of the new age as we generally encountered it in those days was apocalyptic. For all its beauty, wonder, and desirability, it would not or could not come about until after a period of vast planetary social and geological upheaval had "cleansed" the earth of the corrupt old civilizations, thereby giving space for something new to emerge. Therefore, one could believe in a new age, but one could not actively bring it into being, at least not until the apocalypse had come and gone.

No doubt there is some truth in this good millennarian belief, which has been around through most of the history of western civilization. It is naïve in the extreme to think that, given the ordinary resistance of individuals to change, a radical transformation of any society could take place without some kind of upheaval and discontinuity, although the extent and nature of the disruption could well depend on the choices and responses of the people involved. On the other hand, this belief also reflects a fundamental sense of powerlessness. It is a belief that significant change can come about only through the intervention of some nonhuman agency. It has no true participatory element.

Polak's image of the future involved the presence of the Other, which in his terms could be a supernatural agency or the uncharted depths of human creativity and innovation. However, this Other was not necessarily the *source* of the future. Rather it was a *characteristic* of the future, reflecting a need not to make tomorrow simply a mirror of today. The future itself was a product of a creative response on the part of individuals to this Otherness. With a vital image of the future, people remain accountable for participating in its destiny.

The problem with the prophetic new age vision as often conceptualized in the fifties and sixties was that it shifted this accountability away from individual persons and onto the back of vast, impersonal cosmic forces, whether astrological, extraterrestrial, or divine. It took away an individual's sense of being a cocreator with history, of being involved in a process of conscious and participatory evolution. Instead, it encouraged an attitude of waiting for the "Event" that would sweep away the old and usher in the new. This in turn bred a certain attitude of indifference to the world, a sense that "it won't be around all that much longer—therefore, why should I get involved with its problems." Or if the individual chose an activist response to the vision, it often took on a survivalist character: stockpiling food, moving to "safe" locations where the apocalypse wouldn't strike, preparing landing sites for UFO's on rescue missions, and other actions designed to make it through a time of transition but not necessarily to create a new age.

I have always rejected this interpretation of the new age vision. I remember once in Phoenix attending a lecture in which the speaker was holding forth on images of apocalypse, telling in graphic detail what was ahead of us in the way of destruction and warning us to prepare. I became so disturbed at this that without thinking about it I sprang to my feet and shouted, "No! None of what you are saying will happen!" In the silence that followed, as every head in the place turned toward me, the speaker asked, somewhat sarcastically, "Oh? And who's going to stop it? You?" To which I replied "Yes!" and walked out.

From 1965 to 1970, Myrtle and I traveled the "new age circuit," lecturing, holding classes, and offering a counseling service. These were definitely learning years for me, both in observing the many forms that the new age idea and the desire for spiritual growth could take and in discovering and honing my ability to communicate my own thoughts upon these topics. I had very clear and distinct inner experiences upon which to draw for material, but what I lacked was a language—a set of appropriate and simple images—in which to express them. As a consequence, my talks were usually quite abstract and general.

Lecturing itself was not difficult for me. For some years my father had been a toastmaster and had lectured on a variety of subjects from Arab culture to space colonies. I had often gone with him and participated in these events. I had also done some lecturing on my own in school. While I consider myself a basically shy person, I enjoy communicating ideas and establishing a relationship with an audience. I have always had stage fright before a lecture, even now after nearly twenty years of speaking to groups, but when I am actually in front of an audience I feel very relaxed and at home.

I discovered early on that I did not do well working from a prepared text. Using notes or having a prepared talk only made me more nervous, not less. Such aids hampered my ability to establish an empathetic rapport with an audience by competing for my attention. My intent in lecturing has always been simply to share myself, using my own experi-

ences with the spiritual dimension as the basis for my talk.
To accept my fears, my stage fright, and to be vulnerable
to others in order to allow a quality of connectedness to
pass between us was the discipline I had to learn. To be
authentic and honest about my own experience and open to
the moment constitutes the bulk of my preparation. I have
always found that the content I need for a talk is there for
me when required if I have adequately prepared my inner
state first.

However, although the ideas and images might be there
for me if I had attuned myself properly, discovering how
best to express them was another matter. Myrtle had a
specific discipline upon which she could draw, and being
an excellent lecturer, she was always a hit. More importantly, she was understandable. For a time I felt I was getting by largely on the novelty of my youth and subject matter and (or so I liked to believe) on my humor (people
were known to laugh at the appropriate places during my
talks). Myrtle, however, gave our joint presentations concreteness and form and made them relevant to the individual lives of our listeners.

Eventually, I ended up drawing heavily on the images
and cosmologies offered by the esoteric tradition, particularly the writings of theosophy and Alice Bailey, along with
infusions from Christian and Buddhist mysticism, with
some Sufism thrown in for good measure. This served me
for a while and allowed me the time to develop my own
particular images, with the help of some truly exceptional
people who attended my classes in California for a number
of years and became good friends and contributors to my
growth.

During these years that Myrtle and I worked and taught
together, much of our efforts were directly oriented to
changing the pervasive attitude we found of passive waiting for a new age (or something) to happen. Time and
again we encountered sincere and vital individuals who

were living their lives as if someone had pressed a "pause" button. "I feel something big is soon to happen," they would say; "a change is coming, something's in the air, and my life is on hold until it comes. I feel all I can do is wait."

In our work with groups and individuals we sought to extract the essence of the new age idea from its apocalyptic context which, whether it bred fear or passivity, was disempowering. As the decade drew to a close, our work in this regard was greatly enhanced by the very character and sweep of events. The challenge of the flower children and the counterculture and the impact of the civil rights movement and the anti-Vietnam War movement were all being felt then. Likewise, the influx of eastern philosophies and religions was giving new meaning to the nature and practice of spirituality and the human potential movement new meaning to being human.

There were other significant influences on our collective cultural consciousness. There was a growing awareness of ecology, support for "alternative" technologies, the development of concepts of "holistic medicine," and a recognition of feminist issues and the need for articulating and strengthening women's rights. By the end of the decade, as well, there were the Apollo flights to the moon which, through the pictures of earth as seen from space, gave meaning to the concept of one world and one humanity sharing one destiny.

Like some giant new DNA helix, all of these spiritual, social, and technological forces intertwined to give us visions and glimpses of other possible personal and cultural identities. Perhaps most importantly, they offered a sense of participation in history, an experience of the fact that individuals can make a difference. They were forces of empowerment. The idea of the new age dropped like a seed into this milieu of change and exploration in the late sixties and early seventies and began to expand beyond its millennarian roots. The "edge of history" began then to widen into a plateau of new creative vision and efforts.

In 1970, in the midst of this social flux and broadening of vision, Myrtle and I were offered an opportunity to travel to Europe. We both felt that our work was due to take a new turn, but we didn't know in what direction. The chance to spend a few weeks sightseeing and meeting some spiritual groups outside the United States seemed an ideal way to break our routine and give something new a chance to emerge.

Before we left California, I was told in meditation that in Europe we would discover our new work, and I was given a number of signs that would help me recognize when this contact took place. These were not physical signs but rather qualities and connections of which to be aware. Heartened by this information and appropriately alert, we took off for Italy, the first leg of our journey.

Four weeks later we were in London. We had met many wonderful people and had visited some interesting and worthwhile spiritual groups in England, but so far no contact had been made that seemed to open up a new cycle of work for us. In ten days' time we were due to go to Switzerland (which was where I privately expected to find what we were looking for, having a lifelong love affair with mountains and chocolate). In the meantime, we had heard in California of an interesting group in the north of Scotland called the Findhorn community, which was having remarkable results growing a garden on the most barren soil through communication with "nature spirits." It sounded to me like a group of quaint English mediums or spiritualists, and friends of ours in London who seemed to be up on these things said that Findhorn was a center for a lot of psychic nonsense and not to bother with it. We were intrigued, however, and I wrote to the head of the community, Peter Caddy, asking if Myrtle and I could visit. Practically by the next day's mail we received a letter from Peter inviting us up and saying that they had been waiting for two years for me to come. With an introduction like that, how could I resist?

As it turned out, a close friend and coworker of ours in California, May Hanna, had sent Peter and his wife, Eileen, a booklet on spirituality that I had written two years earlier. After reading it, Eileen told us later, she had had a strong feeling that I would one day come to Findhorn. As with many of her feelings about the future, this one proved correct.

Much has already been written and published about Findhorn. When Myrtle and I arrived there in July of 1970, it was only a small group of people living in trailers and bungalows on one half of a trailer park. Started by Peter and Eileen Caddy and Dorothy Maclean in 1962, it was a new age center whose fame had come from its work in developing an amazing garden, where, against all known principles of organic husbandry, the plants grew and thrived in sandy, gravelly soil, exposed to harsh, drying winds off the North Sea. The secret was a mystical relationship which the Caddys, and Dorothy Maclean in particular, had established with the invisible, spiritual, formative forces within nature; through that relationship they were guided in how best to cultivate the garden, but they were also aided in how to develop their own human spirituality and the bonds of a loving, creative community.

Myrtle and I had only been at Findhorn for a day when we both realized that this was the place we had come to find, the contact that would open up our next cycle of work. It fit all the signs for which I had been on the alert. As a consequence, we never did go on to Switzerland. We stayed for three months in the community, returned to the United States to settle up some affairs, and then went back to Findhorn, which became our home for the next two and a half years.

During the time we were there, Findhorn grew from a

small group of about a dozen people to a true community of over one hundred and fifty. Along with Peter, Eileen, and Dorothy, we became codirectors of this center, with a special responsibility for the educational work within the community. While we were there, Findhorn grew not only in size but also in activities, developing, in addition to the work with the garden, studios for pottery, weaving, and other crafts, a performing arts department, a publishing business, and an educational program. It became one of the most creative places I have ever known, and its efforts were focused on discovering and developing models for living that could give substance to the idea of the new age.

This creativity at Findhorn was due in large measure, I believe, to the efforts it made to go beyond its roots. Like many new age groups that were born in the early sixties, it had participated in the millennarian, apocalyptic outlook that I have described, though not as much as some. Not long after we arrived, however, this perspective was directly confronted. Peter Caddy received a letter from a new group in Australia, proclaiming the imminent arrival of the apocalypse and warning other new age groups to prepare themselves. It especially asked Peter to use Findhorn's resources to pass this message along and to stand behind it.

Peter called a meeting of some of us to ask advice on how to respond. Having been dealing in the United States with precisely this issue, both Myrtle and I suggested Findhorn not become aligned with an apocalyptic perspective. This was echoed by others in the group. Since we believed that the new age was not so much an event as a state of mind, it was something we could create and express now, not wait until after some eventual catastrophe. The real questions were not when and how the new age would come but what kind of people we would be when it came and what kind of a world we would wish to build and live in. If we had that vision, then what was stopping us from being that kind of person and working to create that kind of world right now? Instead of spreading warnings of apocalypse, let Findhorn proclaim that the new age is already here, in spirit if not in form, and that anyone can now cocreate with that spirit so that the form will become manifest.

Because all at that meeting felt the same way about this issue, this philosophy of "we are creating the new age now" became Findhorn's policy. It fostered an atmosphere that attracted creative people and nourished their efforts, which is one reason, I believe, why Findhorn has become such a success over the years, even to the point of becoming the archetypal new age center and community. As a model of the new age, it was qualitatively different from the image that I had first encountered in Arizona some fourteen years earlier.

Myrtle and I stayed at Findhorn for three years, then returned to North America in 1973. With us came about a dozen others with whom we had been working in the community (including one special young lady, Julia Manchester, who later became my wife). Having a desire to continue being and working together, we created our own group, the Lorian Association, which we dedicated to the exploration of the spiritual and educational aspects of the new age vision. In identifying ourselves we wished a name that would sound nice but would be meaningless, so that we would not have to deal with any preconceptions and associations around words such as *new age* or *Aquarian*. The word *Lorian* itself simply popped into my mind one day while we were discussing names, and we all liked it, so it stuck.

When Myrtle and I had left for Europe in 1970, the term *new age* had limited associations, some of which we could not identify with, such as its use as an identifying symbol by the so-called drug culture. Upon our return, however, we discovered that this vision had caught on and spread in ways Myrtle and I would not have imagined before we left for Scotland and for the most part had grown and changed for the better in so doing. Like Findhorn, it had outgrown its roots and become a more substantial image of the future.

Since leaving Findhorn, Myrtle and I and the other Lorians have continued to work in various ways among ourselves and with other groups and communities in the United States and Canada to further the birth of a new age. During this time we have seen this idea continue to develop within our culture in both clear and distorted ways. The vision of a new age possesses many facets. It can be seen as a vision of technological progress, as a spiritual renaissance, as a set of strategies for personal and social transformation, as a network of individuals and groups implementing those strategies, as a state of mind, and even as a divine revelation. Each of these facets will be explored in later chapters. Which is the "real" new age depends on the point of view.

In working with many groups and types of activities, however, I have observed that there are certain key ideas in whose absence the image and spirit of the new age cannot truly be said to be present, however much the group may claim otherwise. They represent a revisioning of culture, self, life, and spirituality. To discover and understand these ideas, that their deeper insights may be implemented in the world, is the reason we must journey to the brink.

5

Gaia:
The Ultimate Ecology

I HAVE A BUMPER STICKER ON MY CAR THAT READS, "ONE Earth, One Humanity, One Destiny." It is from an educational organization, Planetary Citizens, on whose board of directors I served for a time. Founded at the beginning of the seventies by Norman Cousins, Donald Keys, and U Thant, the former secretary general of the United Nations, its purpose has been to encourage a practical awareness of our transnational identity, our allegiance to our species, humanity, as well as to our particular country.

Concerning this identity, Dr. John Walsh in a 1973 book, *Intercultural Education in the Community of Man*, affirms that "each human being ought to be introduced simultaneously to two cultures: the one of which he is a part because he was born into a certain cultural grouping, the other of which he is a part because he is a member of the human race." In a section of his book dealing with the "growing realization of the possibility of a community of man," he writes:

> What the philosophers and theologians have spoken of in theory about the community of man or the world community, which before seemed almost pointless, now looms as a real possibility, indeed as a genuine necessity, for both human survival and fulfillment. Technology has made possible what philosophy and theology could only dream of. Human interdependence is now recognized not just as a metaphysical concept but as a psychological and physical fact. Human solidarity may still take a long time to achieve, but almost no one now denies that a true community of man is at least possible.

This possibility of a human culture, a planetary culture, existing side by side in a complementary way with the different historical cultures of humanity, both enriching and being enriched by them, is a central element in the emerging image of the future. In many ways, the phrase *an emerging planetary culture* is replacing the phrase *an emerging new age* among those who are concerned with such things. For example, the Findhorn Foundation community is more likely now to call itself a planetary village than a new age center.

Such rewordings are more than cosmetic. They represent more accurately what is happening. The Findhorn membership is international, and the community has active links and programs with people in many countries around the world. Therefore, it may rightly see itself as a planetary village in the making. The image of a planetary culture also gives greater definition to the idea of a new age, giving it a discernible shape and direction which people can support in specific, concrete ways. It encourages participation, rather than waiting for a possible apocalypse and a nebulous millennium.

The idea of a planetary culture brings very clear images to mind for me. Both Mumford and Walsh speak of such a culture emerging from the existence and activities of individuals for whom the guiding philosophy for behavior is a clear and strong sense of the wholeness of humanity and the interrelatedness and interdependency of all life upon our globe. Mumford calls such an individual the "One World person" or the "united self," while Walsh speaks of the "univérsal person."

If ever there were two people in whom that ideal lives, it is my parents. Growing up in Morocco, I was exposed daily through their lives and actions to the experience of a planetary perspective, for they reached out to explore and to participate in the Moslem and European culture in ways that most other Americans we knew then did not.

Except for the first year, during which time we lived variously in an Arab village, a Corps of Engineers construction camp, a French boarding house, and a hotel in the ancient city of Meknes, we lived on the United States air base of Nouasseur, near Casablanca. Many of our friends let the air base become their world: they had little extended contact with the Arab culture beyond the perimeter fences. This was not so for my parents. For one thing, Dad's job would not permit it. Morocco was a French colony when we first arrived there, but the country was on the brink of a revolution. In order to ascertain the feelings of the Arabs toward the American presence in their country, my father was assigned to contact and establish good relations with various individuals and factions throughout the country. This work took him from the international city of Tangiers in the north to Berber villages and forbidding mud fortresses high in the Atlas Mountains in the south. When he traveled, he usually took my mother and me with him. This in itself was an exposure to different new worlds.

However, my parents' interest in other cultures went far beyond Dad's work. Our home became a multinational center of sorts. I could come home from school and find we were being visited by a British explorer or a French white hunter, a Hungarian freedom fighter or an exiled Rumanian diplomat and friend of Winston Churchill, a Moroccan noble or an Arab gardener. We celebrated Christian and Jewish holidays, as well as Moslem festivals along with our Arab friends.

For my parents, there was really only one faith and one human family, which nevertheless manifested itself as many religions and many national identities. If there was a guiding philosophy in our household, it was Albert Schweitzer's "reverence for all life." Nevertheless, for all their universal feelings, neither of them ever forgot the value and meaning of each separate culture. They always sought to meet each person on his or her own terms, honoring the cultural differences that might be there and respecting that culture for its unique contribution to the world whole. In our own home we deeply honored and celebrated our Christian tradition and heritage as our core faith, but we never lost sight of the planetary context in which that faith exists. In short, my parents fulfilled Walsh's idea that a human being should be seen as part of two cultures—the one into which he or she was born and the one that comes from being "a member of the human race"—and that an understanding of and an allegiance to both must be nourished.

The image of the two cultures is essential, I feel, to the idea of a new age. On the one hand, it expresses the dynamic tension between centralization and decentralization, the group and the individual, the very large and the very small and the need to find a symbiotic relationship between the two. On the other hand, it conveys an understanding essential to the rebirth of the sense of the sacred which is at the heart of the new age. For God is both transcendent and immanent, beyond us and all with which we are familiar and still within us and our everyday world. The sacred draws us past our boundaries into new and unknown territory, yet is accessible to our normal, daily lives. We encounter God in the unique depths of ourselves, and also in the great holistic web of interrelated life, the large context that embraces all faiths, all cultures.

For this reason, for people who seek to explore the terrain of the two cultures, I have always suggested the model my parents made familiar to me: to choose a path or a tradition and become well grounded in it as a tool to explore the depths of oneself and of life, and simultaneously to conduct that exploration and follow that path aware of the larger planetary context. This includes exposure to other faiths and cultural perspectives and an appreciation of their contributions, recognizing that no human path can contain all of God's possibilities and truths. Simply to follow one tradition exclusively is to risk becoming too narrow; to try to follow all of them, taking pieces from each as we see fit, is to risk a superficiality that also denies the sacred. The perspective of the larger whole coupled with the focus of a particular practice has always seemed to me a proper approach. Then, if our practice should prove insufficient after a time, it can naturally unfold into the greater context of a planetary spirituality, much as a flower, securely rooted in the soil, can grow and open to the sun and the larger ecology around it.

The idea of a world culture is an old one. Mystics and philosophers have long recognized the essential unity of the human species, and one of the most ancient human visions is that of the sacred civilization in which all peoples everywhere may live together in harmony and abundance. This vision has been expressed in many ways. For example, a hundred years ago the Bahai faith emerged in the Middle

East, proclaiming the oneness of humanity, the equality of men and women, the essential unity of all religions, and the need to develop a single world government. These were radical ideas then (some of them still are), and the Bahais were the objects of fierce religious persecution, which still persists in Iran.

In recent years, particularly since the Second World War, there have been movements championing a world culture, and the idea has been the subject of numerous books, such as Mumford's or W. Warren Wagar's *Building the City of Man: Outlines of a World Civilization*. I first met Bill Thompson because he stopped at Findhorn in 1972 while traveling around the world doing research on the emergence of a planetary culture. He published his findings a year later under the title *Passages About Earth*.

Unlike many historical expressions of the one-world idea, however, which focus in particular upon the establishment of a world government, the vision of the new age qua planetary civilization arises less out of politics than out of what is called the holistic vision. This is the awareness that all life is interrelated and interdependent, that the formative elements of creation are not bits of matter but relationships, and that evolution is the emergence of ever more complex patterns and syntheses of relationships. A contemporary Jesuit theologian, Thomas Berry, puts it that "every atomic particle is present to every other atomic particle in an inseparable unity, a unity that enables us to say that the volume of each atom is the volume of the universe."

The holistic world view is emerging out of an interesting modern convergence of mysticism and its experience of a universal oneness and science, particularly ecology—which is the science of living relationships—but also physics. It is also being supported by findings in medicine and the healing arts, especially in the mind-body relationship, which has given birth to the holistic health movement. Bill Thompson spoke of this world view in his sermon "On

Food-Sharing, Communion, and Human Culture," given
in November 1981 at the Cathedral of St. John the Divine:
"At its highest, ecology is a resacralization of science, a
new vision of the relationship of the unique part with the
Universal Whole. Just as physics was basic to the engineering of an industrial society, so now ecology is basic to the
stewardship of a new meta-industrial society. In this new
world view the world is not made out of matter, but
music."

In this content, the idea of a planetary culture is less a
political vision than one of creating relatedness, of empowering and nourishing the biological, ecological, and
spiritual relationships that already deeply make us one,
while making accountability to those relationships the guiding factor in our cultural, political, and economic lives. It is
less an image of government than an image of communication and communion, of bringing the music of the human
and natural worlds into harmony.

One who does this in a literal way is Paul Winter and his
musical group, the Paul Winter Consort. In his innovative
records, *Common Ground* and *Callings*, he weaves the
songs and calls of eagles, wolves, whales, dolphins, sea ot-
ters, and harp seals into his human music. These pieces are
haunting and unforgettable. In 1981, Paul was commis-
sioned by the Cathedral of St. John the Divine to compose
a mass celebrating the ecological vision of the wholeness of
the earth. The resulting *Missa Gaia* ("Earth Mass"), using
"the chorus, choristers, and pipe organ of the largest
Gothic cathedral in the world, along with the voices of
wolf, whale, and loon" was first performed on Mother's
Day, 1981, and has since been performed in many different parts of the world.

Gaia is the ancient Greek name for the goddess of the
earth. It is also the name of a recent scientific hypothesis
that has become a crucial element in the idea of a planetary culture. One of the developers of the Gaia hypothesis,

British scientist James Lovelock, describes it in his book
Gaia: "The entire range of living matter on Earth, from
whales to viruses and from oaks to algae, could be regarded as constituting a single living entity, capable of ma-
nipulating the Earth's atmosphere to suit its overall needs
and endowed with faculties and power far beyond those of
its constituent parts." This complex entity, "involving the
Earth's biosphere, atmosphere, oceans, and soil," is what
he defines as Gaia.

There is considerable scientific evidence indicating that
Lovelock is correct in his hypothesis that the Earth is a living being. Beyond science, however, there is a whole religious and mystical tradition that affirms the same idea. The
implications are enormous, requiring us to re-vision the
meaning and context of life as we have come to see it in
western industrial society. If Gaia exists, then we are part
of her, part of a larger life, a greater body of existence, a
wholeness to which we are accountable in our actions.

In a commentary printed with the record album of *Missa
Gaia,* Lovelock himself speaks of this accountability:

> If we are "all creatures great and small," from bacteria to
> whales, part of Gaia, then we are all of us potentially im-
> portant to her well being. We knew in our hearts that
> the destruction of whole ranges of other species was
> wrong but now we know why. No longer can we merely
> regret the passing of one of the great whales, or the blue
> butterfly, nor even the smallpox virus. When we elimi-
> nate one of these from the Earth, we may have destroyed
> a part of ourselves, for we also are a part of Gaia.

In the past, images of a planetary culture have been
strictly anthropomorphic. They have dealt with human issues, with human politics, human economics, human society, as if all else were background to the human drama.
The coming of Gaia changes all that. Gaia is the original,

and ultimately the only, planetary culture. Any human society that does not discover how to fit accountably and harmoniously into that culture cuts itself off both from its source and from its future.

Lovelock speculates that humanity is the evolving nervous system and brain of the planet, the instrumentality through which Gaia becomes self-aware. The purpose of a nervous system is to be the organ of connectedness within and throughout the body and, in a profound way, the organ of service to the well-being and unfoldment of the whole—indeed, it is that which allows the reality and realization of that wholeness to emerge. We have evolved a planetwide system of technological connectedness that can in fact function as a nervous system for humanity, as well as for Gaia. What we have yet to develop is the consciousness and will to see ourselves in such a holistic manner and act accordingly. In the industrial societies, at least, we are as yet a nervous system at war with itself and its body.

A nervous system is a channel for communication within a body, a pathway for the flow of information. However, to be a nervous system is also to have the capacity to think on behalf of the whole body; more precisely, it is to think *as* the whole body. It is the vehicle for an experience of identity.

As Walsh pointed out in the passage quoted earlier (p. 38), the fulfillment of the philosopher's dream of a world community is now made possible by technology. Assisted by orbiting satellites, we can project our eyes and ears nearly anywhere on the globe through television, telephones, and radio. We have global communication, and through the rapidity and comparative ease of modern transportation we have unprecedented global mobility as well.

This technology certainly facilitates a greater experience of our worldwide human identity; at least, it exposes us to cultures different from our own and confronts us with the challenge of expanding our own viewpoints. What this technology does not do is give us an experience of a *planetary* identity, a *Gaian* identity. For all its usefulness and importance as a tool, it does not enable us to think *as* Gaia. It gives us a clearer sense of the nervous system—us—but not of the whole body.

What does it mean to think from the perspective of a planet? This may seem a wholly mystical question—in fact, it can be approached as one. We can, for example, realize that by definition the thoughts and actions of Gaia are toward the nourishment and empowerment of life and its potentialities. Therefore, to think as Gaia—to be Gaia in human form, in other words—is to have an ecological world view. It is to take the well-being of the world and all of its individual parts unto ourselves with compassion and a sense of shared community. It is to honor the importance of relationships and to discern what Gregory Bateson calls "the pattern that connects," the underlying organization that unites all life. It is to act in ways that are empowering and nourishing to the growth of both individual lives and the wholeness they share.

This "thinking as Gaia" is an essential component of Findhorn's perspective. It is the way in which the gardeners there were trained to approach their work with plants, from the plants' and the local ecology's point of view. It is also the perspective behind the emphasis on an empowering and nurturing atmosphere within the community itself. For myself, this kind of thinking evolved out of a series of inner experiences I began having as a child and which have continued throughout my life. I will discuss these more fully in Chapter 7, but basically they constitute a tuning in to, an immersing in, a spirit in which the sense of the interconnections of life comes to the fore and the personal identity merges on a deep level with that of the world itself. In this state, there is no question for me that

Gaia exists, nor that within her is intelligence, purpose, a will to act for the ultimate good of the lives she supports with her body, and a basic alignment with the presence of God.

There are other ways that are not so mystical of learning how to think as Gaia does, to live from the perspective of a planet. In 1976, I was invited by John and Nancy Todd, founders of the New Alchemy Institute, to attend the official dedication by Canadian Prime Minister Pierre Trudeau of the Prince Edward Island Ark. The Ark is an experimental building, known as a bioshelter, combining the elements of a farm, a house, and, through its use of solar and wind power, an electrical generator. Its construction was approved by the provincial government of Prince Edward Island (one of the Maritime Provinces) as an alternative to a nuclear reactor, and on the day it opened it did indeed feed energy back into the island's power network.

The Ark is located at the tip of a windswept peninsula, only a few hundred feet from a cliff that overlooks the Atlantic Ocean to the south and east. At one point during the celebrations I walked out to that cliff by myself and looked back. It was a moment similar to the time I had sat on stage with astronaut Rusty Schweickart, at the same Lindisfarne Fellows conference where I had first met the Todds. This time there were no flashbacks to my father or grandfather, but rather a flash forward or perhaps a flash sideways. The entire south face of the Ark is covered in glass and solar panels. As I stood there, it caught the light of the sun and sky and was simply transformed into a building of light. It became ethereal, a temple of fire from some other dimension momentarily descended to earth, and I felt myself transported into a place of rapture, a mythic realm where all the earth sang in a unity of joy. The Ark seemed to be the outpost of a true planetary culture.

In *Tomorrow Is Our Permanent Address* the Todds describe a bioshelter and the particular consciousness it can engender:

> [The term *bioshelter*] refers to a building housing a contained and miniaturized ecosystem. Relying on and responsive to the sun as its primary energy source, it is comparable to an organism in that it functions as a membrane between an inner and outer world, both living, whereas standard buildings are more like shells enclosing an artificial, static environment. A bioshelter is a growing structure in which such living components as microorganisms, vegetables, herbs, trees, fruits, flowers, insects, lizards, toads, and people interact to regulate the atmosphere, climate, and productivity of the whole.
>
> Beyond the concrete advantages implicit in the adoption of the bioshelter on a significant scale . . . there is yet another hopeful possibility, that of a perceptual change. . . . Paradoxically, although it is derived from technology, the bioshelter removes the barrier between the human and the other living elements in the system. . . . Working or living in a bioshelter can provide a setting for a renewed intimacy between ourselves and the forces that ultimately sustain us. . . . We begin to see that we are dealing with a multidimensional web of forces, all of which affect and interact with each other.

In short, we begin to see with the perspective of Gaia. Living in a bioshelter, one becomes involved directly in sustaining a mini-ecology. To fail to do so is to disrupt the very systems on which the well-being of the house itself depends. What is this but a miniaturized model of how we should participate within and act toward the planetary ecology in which we live?

The bioshelter is a mythic construct as well as a practical, ecological one. It is a portal into the mind of Gaia, a rite of identification with the processes of Earth, a symbol of how we may learn to think, not just *about* a planet, but *as* a planet. It is part of the knowledge we need in order to incarnate the planetary culture that is Gaia.

Even if Lovelock (and thousands of mystics, shamans, prophets, poets, philosophers, farmers, and lovers of nature) are wrong and a vast planetary being such as Gaia does not exist, it would change nothing. If nothing else, Gaia is the embodiment of the ecological ethic, and as such she is an idea whose time has come.

The idea of ecology, however, must be more than just a notion of conservation practices and world resource management. It must transcend the anthropomorphic and become "Gaiamorphic." Even some new age advocates fail to see this, assuming that in the light of a "new consciousness," we will know how to transform the world and make it a paradise, continuing in this assumption the basic paradigm of humanity acting upon the world as a separate object because we know best what its destiny should be.

A world culture must not only serve human interests but must nurture the potential and well-being of all planetary life. Further, it must do so as part of nature, not as something aloof and separate from it. It is an expression of the whole of nature, not just a human point of view. The image of Gaia restores us to being part of an Earth community, first among equals perhaps but only because of our potentially greater ability to understand and serve the whole. By giving us a deeper insight into the connectedness of life, it can throw new light on our common destiny, mutually arrived at.

To violate Gaia is ultimately to violate ourselves; to nourish her is to be nourished. We are truly, as my bumper sticker proclaims, "One Earth, One Humanity, One Destiny." While *culture* can mean the arts and crafts of civilization, the verb *to culture* means to nourish and to culti-

vate. Thus, the idea of a planetary culture also suggests our
capacity to participate in the culturing of our world until
she—and we—can emerge, pearl-like in our wholeness, from
the irritants that now beset us.

6

The Spacesuit and the Cathedral

ONE OF THE GREAT PLEASURES OF MY LIFE HAS BEEN MY growing association with the Cathedral of St. John the Divine in New York City. A very large part of this pleasure is in knowing the Very Reverend James Parks Morton, dean of the cathedral. A great loving, vibrant bear of a man, Jim puts the lie to any idea that a cleric is somehow "otherworldly" or that a deep spirituality cannot be combined with the daily round of a down-to-earth life.

We have been acquaintances for some years, meeting annually at Lindisfarne Fellows conferences, and we both serve on the Board of Advisors for John Denver's Windstar Community in Snowmass, Colorado. However, I really got to know him and his wife, Pamela, during the summer of 1981, when we lectured together at a week-long conference on the new age and the future of Christianity. It was at that time that we developed a plan to draw a number of new age centers and communities together for a conference at the cathedral.

Ultimately, the conference was jointly set up by the cathedral, by the Lorian Association, and by the Chinook Learning Community, an educational center located on Whidbey Island in Puget Sound, near Seattle. Called "The Earth Community: A Coming of Age," it presented to the public for the first time the combined work of a number of allied groups, including the New Alchemy Institute, Windstar, the High Wind Association, an educational and ecological community in Wisconsin, and Columcille, a spiritual retreat center in eastern Pennsylvania. The intent was to show a wide range of activities, from communities to schools to religious centers, that had coalesced under the banner of the new age, cultural transformation, and reverence for Gaia. Throughout the day the Cathedral Players, led by John Michael Tebelak, the creator of *Godspell*, gave counterpoint to the lectures by acting out the story of Noah and an earlier transformation, dancing and singing to music composed by my Lorian colleague Milenko Matanovic. This production culminated in a magical late-night procession from the Synod House a block away up Amsterdam Avenue into the cathedral itself and up to the high altar, singing one of Milenko's songs, "Festival of Light."

The conference was reasonably successful and, thanks to the Cathedral Players, a great deal of fun. It also fulfilled the purpose of bringing together the leaders of a number of groups to become better acquainted. What made the event different for me, though, took place a week later. During the conference Dean Morton had casually invited anyone who was interested in pursuing the idea further to come to a meeting the following week. Much to his amazement, over a hundred and thirty people showed up, all wanting to start a new age center based at the cathedral, to explore community, ecology, and spirituality and to sponsor service projects for people in the city of New York. Jim was more than happy for this to take place, but the next day both Milenko and I received phone calls from him saying, "You started this, now come and help us out!" As a consequence, for the following year we both traveled to the cathedral as often as we could to meet with the dean and with this evolving group of people, who call themselves the Earth Community, after the conference that got them started.

That an Episcopal cathedral, the world's largest Gothic structure, should be the home of a new age group, most of whose members are not even Episcopalian, may seem strange, but it is in keeping with the history and nature of cathedrals themselves. (It is also in harmony with the ecumenical and universal spirit of Dean Morton and his wife.) Cathedrals have always been close to the heart of western culture, places of innovation and cultural development, sacred centers around which cities grew and from which universities emerged. While upholding tradition, they have often also provided the spiritual, intellectual, and artistic impetus for transformation. In their architecture and design they embody our feelings of transcendence, our relationship with the Other who is at the center of a true image of the future. British architect Keith Critchlow, an expert on sacred geometry, describes this relationship: "The cross of the cathedral is the cube, symbol of material perfection, unfolded. . . . It is the exploding of the imprisonment of the material plane by the Spirit, allowing the soul to be released."

This liberation, this openness to new possibilities that the spirit can bring by "exploding" the limitations of the material plane, is an eloquent definition of the sacred. It is not a liberation from the world but a freedom secured by unfolding the potentials within the world. It is precisely this freedom that a true image of the future offers, for it liberates us from the imprisonment of habit and the limitations of the familiar. It offers transcendence of the known in ways that honor and extend the known. It is not escape. It is empowerment and fulfillment. Thus, the cathedral is an "explosion in stone." Its structure symbolizes the freedom of the spirit paradoxically contained, not dispersed but turned into a source of energy for the empowerment and nourishment of life.

The desire for this liberation is strong in our society. It is a hunger for transcendence that I often encounter in my travels and lectures. It is one of the motivations that draws people into considering the idea of the new age, for almost by definition this idea offers transcendence and liberation from the world as we know it, which for many people is frightening, depressing, and dangerous. Unfortunately, in the quest for the transcendent, for a renewed connection with the sacred at the heart of all true culture, we may opt for escape instead.

In July 1969, I joined millions of other people around the world to watch the first moon walk on television. "The *Eagle* has landed!" we heard, and Neil Armstrong emerged from *Apollo 11* to make his "one small step for a man, one giant leap for mankind." As the descendant of a man who launched homemade rockets from the Ohio hills and another who filled the house with both science and science fiction and regaled me with speculations about life Out There, I was properly thrilled. From the orbital hop of John Glenn onward, I have been a fan of the space program, and both astronauts and cosmonauts have a special place in my private pantheon of heroes. If ever they have a place on a space shuttle for an itinerant mystic and new age prophet, I shall definitely place my name on the list.

For many people, space and the new age are practically synonymous. In books such as *The Third Industrial Revolution* by G. Harry Stine, *The Evolutionary Journey* by Barbara Marx Hubbard, and *Doomsday Has Been Cancelled* by J. Peter Vajk, projects such as the creation of space colonies and the shifting of industries into near earth orbit are seen as doorways into a new world of abundance for humanity. They are also seen as the means for transforming ourselves from a limited, planet-bound species into a cosmic one—the logical next step, in the view of Vajk and Hubbard, both for humanity and for Gaia. They are acts of transcendence.

There may well be practical economic reasons for developing the potentials of space, although Daniel Deudney, a senior researcher for the Worldwatch Institute in Washington, D.C., refutes the value and feasibility of some of the more glamorous projects, such as space colonies, in his publication *Space: The High Frontier in Perspective*. Unfortunately, we know there are military reasons as well, which apparently are being explored by both the United States and the Soviet Union. However, the feeling I observe behind much of the talk about the development of space is as much religious in its tone as it is pragmatic. It is as if for some people the space program is a modern equivalent of the aspiration for the transcendental that empowered the great cathedral-building projects of the Middle Ages. It is our way of reaching toward the heavens, metaphorically as well as literally.

As something to fill the void of the sacred, however, the space program is insufficient. Using a chemical reaction to propel men inside a steel container into a vacuum is an event, however glamorous and useful it may be. A cathedral is a presence and a process. It is at its best a seed that gives life to the world around it. As an image of liberation, space exploration, at the present time at least, is more an image of escape. It is flawed transcendence because it is that alone. It is essentially a going out, not a return. It does not fulfill or honor the earth.

The cathedrals, on the other hand, were—and are, or can be—a celebration of the sacred united with the earth, growing out of the earth, entering into the earth. They are examples of grounded transcendence, of incarnate liberation. The space program will be like a cathedral, a true and worthy vessel for meeting the human hunger for transcendence and the sacred, only when it can inspire reverence for our own planet with the same enthusiasm and dedication with which it seeks other worlds, leading us to honor and serve Gaia and her enfolded potentials as a living world and not regard her just as a launching pad for somewhere else.

The space program is not the only kind of exploration that can be a form of escape while appearing to be a path of transcendence. The quests for spirituality and for a liberated self can also be misused. At their highest, the revisioning of the meaning of the sacred and the nature of the human self are the third and fourth key elements within the idea of the new age, the first two being the emergence of planetary culture and the recognition of Gaia. However, in a lesser form, they can become, like the space program at its worst, images of escape.

There is an important revisioning of spirituality going on—a new interest in the nature of the sacred dimension of life. Ironically, much of the impetus for this revisioning has come from modern sciences, such as physics and ecology, which are revealing a universe that is an unbroken wholeness, not unlike the vision of the mystic. At the same time, as cultures converge, we are experiencing an increasing cross-pollination between the religions of the world. This can lead to doctrinal difficulties and conflicts, but it also leads to a deepening realization of what Frithjof Schuon calls "the transcendent unity of religions." In his book by that title, he discusses the common root experience of the sacred that lies at the source of all religious expression and demonstrates the unity of these religions within what he calls the "esoteric" or essential domain of existence. Similarly, there is a perennial philosophy, as Aldous Huxley

named it, a body of insights, teachings, wisdom, and experience that can be found in almost identical form in nearly
every culture of humanity. These insights transcend religious differences and provide a basis for a planetary spirituality.

At the same time, the idea of planetary spirituality takes
on an even broader meaning when considered in the context of Gaia. What is the spiritual nature of our planet?
How does humanity relate to it? The Findhorn garden was
based on communication with precisely that nature, not in
a worshipful or pantheistic sense of seeing nature as God,
but rather in recognition that nature, too, has a soul with
which we may share a communion of mutual interests as
children of God. Findhorn is part of a spiritual tradition,
which can be found in many religions including Christianity (particularly in Celtic Christianity and in the work
of the German mystic, Meister Eckhart) that could be
called creation theology. In this tradition humanity participates in and is even responsible for the spiritual unfoldment of the earth, of nature, and of matter itself, as well as
of its own spiritual progress.

The quest for the meaning of planetary spirituality is, to
me, a necessary component of the new age idea. Unfortunately, the lesser side of this quest becomes a search for experiences, particularly of a psychic nature. This is largely
due to a convergence of spiritual illiteracy in our culture
with a public interest, semisupported by scientific research,
in extrasensory perception. The new age circuit is filled
with groups and teachers offering classes and weekend
seminars on how to become psychic.

Having a background of psychic and mystical experiences, I know that the human mind and soul are capable of
far more than an exclusively materialistic model of the universe would allow. I fully believe that parapsychological
research and the skillful and appropriate development of
extended sensory abilities are worthy areas of exploration.

Like the space program, however, psychic phenomena are a poor vessel to contain our longing for the transcendent; they are an inappropriate substitute for the experience of the sacred. They represent refined forms of sensory experience which can "explode" our minds by putting us in touch with an aspect of the universe different from the physical and which we may not have known existed, but they cannot liberate our souls. Psychic powers do not create cathedrals. They can, however, effectively launch our consciousnesses out of this world and can serve as a glamorous form of escape when not integrated into the discipline of an ordinary material life.

Similar pitfalls surround our quest for a new vision of selfhood. The indulgences of the "me decade" and the narcissistic excesses of the human potential movement have been so frequently analyzed and criticized as to be clichés. Humanistic and transpersonal psychologies have done much to open us to new vistas of inner creative possibilities and talents. Nevertheless, in the pop psychology versions of these disciplines, the concept of the "real self" emerges as the criterion against which all experience must be measured. Does this relationship, this job, this situation help me discover, unfold, nourish, develop my real self? And what is this real self, the holy grail for which so many knights go questing through the rigors of weekend seminars and sensitivity training classes? Again, it is a modern substitute for the image of the sacred, the point of transcendence, the point of liberation. It becomes a new deity, to which we are often willing to sacrifice everything on the altar of growth and personal fulfillment, for if we can connect with it, it promises us liberation. What it delivers, though, is only the illusion of escape, for like psychic powers, this ego masquerading as the real self cannot release us into the world and from imprisonment. It, too, cannot build a cathedral.

Once more, it is the loss in our culture of a true sense of the sacred that opens us to distortions. It is important that we discover a new vision of who we are. For too long we have suffered under very limiting images of our human nature and potentials, not the least damaging of which is our current image of a person as essentially an economic entity —a consumer and a replacement part in the industrial social machine. As part of the emergence which the new age idea proclaims, we recollect ourselves as creative and cocreative individuals, as embodiments of a sacred self.

As part of this recollection, though, we must also remember that the true "real self," the sacred identity within us, is not a thing, an object unto itself; it is a condition of connectedness and mutuality, of love and of community; it is a process, an accessibility, an accountability, an empowerment, and a sharing.

The space program, psychic development in the name of spirituality, and the quest for growth and the real self are all alike. They all seem to offer transcendence and liberation, but what they deliver is more confinement. Each is finally an image of isolation. Each requires that we take our familiar environment with us essentially unchanged, like the astronaut in his spacesuit. The spacesuit miniaturizes the world so that the spaceman can take it along with him, but within it he remains separate from the universe around him. He may have new experiences, but he is not transformed into a different creature. He does not learn to become a being of energy, capable of surviving in space and riding the cosmic waves of light between the stars.

But transformation, rebirth into a different creature, a new life, is what the sacred dimension is all about. It is the essence of the new age idea: exposure to that which changes, to that which explodes and unfolds you. It is the message of the cathedral, and it is precisely this discovery of the self and the spirit as cathedrals and not spacesuits that will bring a new age into being.

7

Delving Inward

IT IS 1952, AND I AM SEVEN YEARS OLD. ON THIS PARTICULAR day my parents and I are driving from the air base of Nouasseur to the nearby city of Casablanca on a shopping expedition. It is a journey we have made many times before, and I am sitting in the back seat of our car idly watching the scenery go by.

All at once I am filled with a feeling of energy coursing through my body and a sensation as if I am expanding like a balloon. Before I can think about what is happening, I find myself somehow outside my body but enveloping it. Looking down and in some fashion within at the same time, I see my physical form, my parents and our automobile, tiny objects rapidly shrinking out of view. When they

are gone, I am alone in an unbroken field of white
light. . . .

In this manner, there began one of the most powerful
and important experiences of my life. It came upon me un-
expectedly, lasted for what seemed like hours (though in
actuality it was only a few seconds), and left me with a
different vision of reality than I had had before.

The experience went through four distinct stages. The
first was a feeling of reawakening, as if I had been asleep.
What I awakened to was a sense of identity, not as David
Spangler, a finite, earthly personality, but as pure being, at
one with the light around me, at one with creation. Along
with this came an exhilaration, a feeling of release and joy
as boundaries fell away.

Then the light cleared, in a manner of speaking, and I
entered a second stage: I could "see" myself (though an
act of visual perception was not quite what was taking
place). However, this "self" that I saw was not a body but
a pattern at the center of which was I as the observer.
Within this pattern were other personalities, some of which
I could discern as physical forms but most of which, as
near as I can describe it, appeared as configurations of
qualities. In that moment I knew that these were other aspects of me, other lives and experiences that I had had or
would likely yet have in what, to my earthly personality,
would be the future. At the same time, I had flashes of
memories of births and deaths that I had known, and while
no particular historical personalities stood out, what did
emerge was a clear perception of the eternity of the soul
and the continuity of self beyond the physical dimension.

To this point, the whole experience was exactly as if I
had awakened in a strange but familiar room and was looking around to orient myself. It was an experience of re-
membering, of recollecting myself in the purest sense of
that word. Once I was oriented, however, conditions
changed and I entered the third stage. The pattern of lives,

even the surrounding light, all disappeared. In its place I found myself in a state I cannot describe visually except to say that I was embraced by a great presence. In this presence, all things seemed to exist in a profound oneness, filled with an indescribable love and serenity and with an irresistible power as well.

As if a curtain were drawn aside, I had a visual impression of the universe, a great wheel of stars and galaxies, suffused with the golden glow of billions of suns, floating in a sea of spirit. It was as if I were seeing as this presence saw, and for one instant we were as one. In that instant, it was as if I were one with everything that existed, every atom, every stone, every world, every star, seeing creation not from some great distance but from the inside out as if it were my very body and being. Even more powerful than this perception was the awareness of the flow of creativity throughout everything I saw and the joyous embrace of life and unfoldment in response; the rhythm was that of a ballroom, with its music and its dancers and the intricate patterns they all created, ever changing, ever unfolding.

Then the experience entered its last stage. Swept up by this cosmic dance, so to speak, I found myself looking down at the earth and then upon myself as David. In that instant I felt the intent to be David, the will to be born that had precipitated my current personality and physical life into being. I felt the connectedness of that intent to all the other patterns unfolding in creation and what I can only describe as the rightness of being born. With that came a sensation of great love, not only for David but for all manifestations of human life, for the whole drama and purpose of human existence, for the choice that each soul makes to incarnate and be part of the dance on this particular planet. Then, swept up in the power of that intent and love, I seemed to move forward, and the next I knew I was back in my body, still staring out the window.

This experience left me with two lasting impressions that

have influenced my life since then. The first is an awareness of a spirit of life and creativity within all that is and of my connectedness with that spirit. It is a perception of the presence of God within creation and the wholeness that presence imparts. The second is an awareness of—and sensitivity to—another part of myself, one that is vastly more expansive than my personality; it is a deeper self, one that participates in eternity even as my daily self participates in time.

While I was growing up, these two impressions formed part of the background of my life. Though I didn't talk about this experience much with my parents at the time, their own attitudes and way of life, so embracing and universal in outlook, created an environment fully in harmony with its character. Further, one of the dominant feelings throughout that experience was one of complete naturalness. As a consequence, I simply accepted as normal the perspective these impressions gave me and went on about the business of growing up without giving much more thought to what had happened.

After we moved to Phoenix, however, and became involved with people specifically studying mystical and psychic phenomena, I began to reflect more on that event. I sought to work with the impressions it had given me in a more deliberate way, including learning meditation in order to have a more conscious contact with the "other" part of me. It was out of that study and discipline that I began gaining insights into what I called the spiritual worlds and into processes of spiritual development, insights that later formed the material for my career as a lecturer. It was from this, as well, that my involvement with the idea of a new age grew. Among the first fruits of my delving inward was the connection with a "flow" or "intent" of spirit, a sense that something was to emerge in our time. It was an experience of Mumford's "brink" or Bill Thompson's "edge," a prophetic sense of the manifestation of the sacred dimension of life in human history.

This insight allowed me to say yes to the idea of a new age, even when that idea was presented to me in forms I could not accept. It also led me to leave college in 1965 and become part of the new age subculture of that era. However, my personal motivation has not been as much toward transformation for its own sake as toward an exploration of the sacred and its relationship to our personal and cultural lives. For me, the new age has always been less an image of change and more an image of spiritual deepening.

My inward delvings took another turn that summer I left home and Myrtle and I began working together. We had been invited to lecture and give classes at a spiritual center in Los Angeles run by two friends of ours, Wayne Guthrie and Bella Karish. Both Wayne and Bella are gifted psychics who bring a high level of integrity, skill, and balance to their work and service. I have already said that Myrtle and I entered the circuit of new age, esoteric, psychic, and metaphysical groups like babes entering a forest. For the first couple of years of our work, Wayne and Bella were our wise guides and supportve friends who, avoiding much of the distortion and glamour to be found on that circuit, made our way much safer and easier.

In the first month we were in Los Angeles, Myrtle and I stayed with Bella in a very large and roomy house she was sharing with a friend. One morning, after everyone else had gone to work, Myrtle and I were sitting in the living room, discussing our plans for the day. I remember it was one of those hot, smog-filled Los Angeles days, and neither of us was in a hurry to stir from the coolness of the house. While talking, I felt strongly that someone had walked into the room. This person's presence was overwhelming, though in fact there was no one else physically with us. In my inner work to that time, I had occasionally been aware of and made contact with invisible, spiritual beings. Such phenomena came with the territory I was investigating. However, I had never before felt such a strong and immediate presence.

I shared this perception with Myrtle, and after discussing it briefly we agreed to sit in meditation to attempt a contact with this being. My method of doing this is to shift the focus of my consciousness and my attention to my other, deeper self, the one I had opened to when I was seven. Although this results in a change of perception, I do not enter anything like a trance state. I remain fully conscious of myself and my surroundings, though my attention is detached. In this state, however, I do become more conscious of my inner self and the world within which it functions.

When I entered this state at that time, not only did I become immediately aware of this other individual in the room but I felt my inner being and his uniting in a very deep way that I had not experienced before. It was like two old friends greeting and embracing each other in love. I then realized that through the connection we had formed, we could communicate through a blending of thoughts, feelings, and images. Though this was an inner communion, I spoke his thoughts out loud so that Myrtle could know what was happening and what was being said.

That first contact was brief. The individual introduced himself as an old friend and colleague of ours who, now that we had come together, was joining us again to be a partner in our work. He said that in his present state of being his name was a quality of vibration, but that we could call him John, as it was "as good a name as any."

Thus began a relationship with a spiritual being that continues to this day. In the beginning, as part of a training program, John would come to us twice a day, during which time I learned through him to hone my skills at working with the inner dimensions of spirit. Then the intensity of our contact tapered off as our work together became easier and more adroit. Over the years since then, John has come and gone. Sometimes, when the situation demands it, he works with us regularly, while at other times months may pass with little communication between us. During that time we have collected well over a thousand pages of transcripts of discussions between us on a variety of subjects. Some of these Lorian has published in two booklets—*Conversations with John,* which basically deals with politics and world affairs, and *Cooperation with Spirit,* which offers John's insights into his own world and work and his perspective on how our two worlds may cooperate.

In this regard he is a staunch advocate of mutual empowerment and freedom from dependency. From the beginning of our association together, John has stressed that he was not a "guide" in any spiritualistic sense and that we could not look to him to tell us what to do. If anything, he was here to strengthen our capacity to decide for ourselves and to make skillful use of our God-given faculties of intelligence and free will. He stated that he was with us as a friend and coworker whose main contribution was to offer us his perspective on life. This was the perspective I have called holistic, for John lives in the world I briefly touched when I was seven, a world defined by the connectedness and interrelatedness of things, in which the loving spirit of God is everywhere present. If we could learn to see reality as he did, then we would not need him to give us direction; we would know what to do ourselves. Whatever he told us, we were asked to think it through for ourselves and determine if the information both rang true for us and was useful in our lives. This approach suited us fine, for both Myrtle and I believe strongly in empowering individuals to be interdependent, not dependent.

Over the years it has been evident that John's main interest is the emergence of a new age and a new culture, and he identifies himself as one of those on the spiritual side of life whose work is specifically to empower that emergence.

Many of my own insights in this area come out of my association with John. However, in no respect are Myrtle and I
John's "agents" on earth, simply passing on his perspectives. We are more precisely colleagues whose work moves
in the same direction toward the same goals and who can
therefore share the fruits of our mutual labors.

Working with John has been an education in itself in
understanding the need and the search for the sacred. It
has been particularly enlightening to observe how people
respond to him and to the phenomenon of our communication together, and to realize the mystique and glamour that can distort the idea of contact with spiritual
worlds. John has always been clear that working with his
world, however transcendental it may seem, does not meet
the need of the evolving spirit for transcendence. It is no
substitute for communion with the sacred. It is simply a
connection with another part of the universe, important in
giving us a sense of the vaster community of life of which
we are a part but not to be confused with touching the
inner heart of that community, which is God.

The experiences I have had of a mystical nature or of
working with John and his colleagues naturally give me a
bias. I could not write a book on the new age without making that bias clear. I do not approach this subject as a sociologist or futurist, a journalist or historian, however important and necessary the contributions of these and other
professions may be in discussing the idea of cultural transformation. I write as someone in the midst of an ongoing
spiritual discipline, sharing travel notes while journeying
along the brink.

The holistic universe is a reality, and from its center God
works to open up humanity to a fuller experience of that
reality. We are on the verge—indeed, in the midst of—a
new revelation of spirit and the sacred on behalf of our
long-suffering world. Because I have experienced this as

the central spiritual fact of our time, the new age is no theory to me, nor just a possible image of the future. It exists as a present and ongoing transformation, however imperfectly we may apprehend it.

8

Labor Pains

THE IDEA OF A NEW AGE EXISTS AS SOMETHING MORE THAN JUST
a prophetic vision precisely because in our time change and
transformation have become credible concepts. Up until
fairly recently in human history, changes in society took
place over long periods of time; generations might pass
without any significant or apparent signs of transformation.
Now the experience of change is everywhere. Only eighty
years have passed since the Wright brothers made their
first flight at Kitty Hawk and Henry Ford opened his first
factory. How greatly just those two events have changed
our lives! In my lifetime we have seen the introduction of
atomic energy, television, space travel, global satellite communications, and transistors, the discovery of the DNA
double helix and the beginning of genetic engineering, and

the recent development of the silicon microchip, making possible a whole new electronics revolution based on ultra-miniaturization.

This latter change is especially mirrored in the development of computers. The first successful computer, ENIAC, was built in 1946, the year after I was born. It weighed thirty tons and cost over half a million 1950 dollars; it was also not very efficient at first, breaking down about every ten minutes. Today, I am writing this chapter on an Apple II microcomputer word programmer, which, being smaller than an IBM typewriter, fits comfortably on my desk. It offers me at least the same amount of computing power as the ENIAC and cost less than fifteen hundred 1982 dollars. It is also vastly more efficient: it can keep going, but eventually I have to stop to eat, sleep, and rediscover the world outside my study.

These changes I have mentioned are all technological. Technology is often the most visible reflection of change in our lives and as such is useful for illustrating my point. There have been profound social, political, and economic changes over the past eighty years, as well. For example, the Soviet Union did not exist (nor, for that matter, did most of the nations in the world today) when many of the people now alive were born.

The effect of this is to give all of us a living experience of transformation which was rarely available to earlier generations of humanity. We perceive the world in flux, even more so as time goes along. As a consequence, the idea that we are on the brink of a new age is not such an unreasonable notion as it might once have been. If anything, it has almost become a cliché. What many people have difficulty with, I have discovered, is not the idea that transformation is taking place but that it will result in a better future. It is the optimistic flavor of the new age idea that seems incredible now.

Looking at the challenges that beset our world, from nuclear weapons to ecological degradation, from mass poverty and starvation among most of the globe's population to the political and economic instabilities this causes, it is easy to see why an attitude of pessimism would seem the most reasonable approach to the future.

At SRI International, a research institute located in Menlo Park, California, a project group has spent more than a decade studying the possible futures before us. Three members of this group—Paul Hawken, James Ogilvy, and Peter Schwartz—have shared some of their findings and suggestions in a book called *Seven Tomorrows:*

> The coming decades are likely to be a watershed, a time that will change much that we hold familiar. While the Hydra-headed problems of reduced energy, rising hunger, increasingly erratic weather, and constant global conflict augur poorly for our collective fate, we do not see that fate as inevitable or the problems as insoluble. The one resource that is boundless and abundant in all our futures is the human spirit. Of all the variables that one must consider when looking ahead, it is the one that remains positive. Ultimately, the future of our country and our planet does not lie solely in external events, but also with the will of its inhabitants.

The issue is one of motivation. We live in a time of great flux, out of which, as the researchers at SRI indicate, a number of different futures could possibly emerge. What does emerge—and with what grace or trauma—is greatly up to us, the visions we embrace, the choices we make. What images call forth our highest and noblest efforts? What future can we call forth, in turn? There is much pain and suffering in the world. Is there more now than ever before? There are more people now, and our ability to communicate the images of suffering are vastly enhanced, thereby increasing our awareness of the pain in our world. For many people that awareness itself is threatening, leading to attempts to escape by ignoring it or by muffling it in swaths of despair and pessimism. There is no question but that this pain and suffering can multiply, perhaps ultimately to cover the earth physically, even as it does now psychically. What will motivate us to prevent that and change the situation? Images of death? Or of birth?

The idea of transformation tends to generate dramatic images: the rise of charismatic leaders, the march of multitudes on behalf of a new vision, the catastrophic event that sweeps the old order away practically overnight. It has been my observation, however, that the essence of the transformative journey lies in its small and ordinary steps: a change of diet, perhaps, or giving ten minutes a day over to meditation, a willingness to be open to new points of view or an effort to heal conflicts in our lives. The emergence of a new culture comes from hundreds of thousands of such small, anonymous acts that collectively exert an influence. For example, I can remember a time not so long ago when to see someone out running or jogging was an unusual sight. Now several runners a day pass by my house, usually in packs, and hardly anyone pays them any attention. Yet no one leader is responsible for the spread of this new kind of exercise in our culture. It has emerged from a growing collective response to an idea.

There are transformative movements that spread recognizably and quickly from the work of single individuals and groups. Examples of this are seen in the work of Dr. Fernand Lamaze and Dr. Frederick Leboyer in changing American perspectives on the birthing process and in the equally persuasive work of Dr. Elisabeth Kübler-Ross in changing how we deal with death, the other end of the natural biological cycle.

Most transformational work is less public. It is the application of new values and new visions to the details and trivia of our everyday lives. In trying something new, we may meet misunderstanding and opposition from friends and families and may feel ourselves isolated. Also, it may take time before any results of our efforts appear. Peter and

Eileen Caddy and Dorothy Maclean lived and worked together for nearly eight years before the Findhorn community began to emerge from their efforts; Fritz and Vivienne
Hull lived on an old abandoned farm without electricity or
plumbing for several years, rebuilding and transforming it,
before it became the center for the thriving Chinook
Learning Community. In both cases, these people had to
make personal sacrifices, give up jobs, even lose friends in
order to follow their visions of transformation, and the final
good results of their efforts have been based on a solid
foundation of very ordinary, unglamorous work and attention to the details of physical labor, spiritual practice, loving relationships, and an openness to learning.

Transformation does not always demand that we lose
jobs or friends; the glamour of martyrdom is attractive to
some kinds of people for whom a sense of being persecuted
or rejected by society is nourishment for their egos. Transformative work does require a willingness to take appropriate and balanced actions on behalf of a new vision, and
these can on occasion entail sacrifice. More importantly, I
feel, this work requires a long-term vision, a willingness to
buckle down for the long haul and not expect to see the
final results overnight or even in our lifetimes. It requires a
deep commitment. It requires a vision that can inspire and
get us through the periods of struggle and loneliness. The
image of a dismal future, without hope, perhaps even without life, cannot provide this.

For this reason, I see the new age as a vision of birth,
and have always presented it as such in my work. A birth is
a glorious event, but it is one often accompanied by the
travail and the pain of labor. One can look at the travail
going on in the world, therefore, and see it not only as the
death of an old civilization but as the labor pains of a new
one.

As every parent knows, births are participatory events.
People are involved in bringing them about; further, once
the baby appears, the work really begins! It is true that

some versions of the new age vision, particularly in its more millennarian and apocalyptic forms, convey a sense of some larger force taking care of our future for us. There is an optimism that disclaims the need to work for change because God or spiritual adepts or flying saucers will somehow accomplish the transformation for us. This is merely withdrawal, a failure of motivation because of a fear of the future and a sense of powerlessness.

The new age is not guaranteed; an optimism based on a feeling of inevitability may only lessen our ability to enter into the work necessary to bring a different culture into being. The new age is, instead, an image that can motivate us to act and work for a transformed future, one that is humane, decent, and abundant, a credit to humanity and a blessing to the earth. We are part of that which can make a difference. Because we are capable of choice and will and action on behalf of a positive vision, there is valid reason for optimism.

The idea of the new age, as I see it, is—and must be—an optimistic vision. It cannot be anything other. It is not a vision of nuclear holocaust nor of ecological degradation nor of social collapse, though it must take these possibilities into account and invoke the human energy necessary to direct our future away from them. Consequently, a person who seeks to serve or embody this idea must himself or herself be birth-oriented, not haunted or obsessed with images of destruction. There is too much fear in the world already, poisoning our efforts at healing and change, for those who seek to shape our future to add to the burden. Instead, such a person must be able to marshal our positive wills and our creative responses to exorcise these demons on behalf of a loving transformation.

If the acceleration of change in our century has made it possible for us to accept the idea of transformation, then the image of birth can strengthen our resolve. We are, as Rusty Schweickart said, "sensing elements" for the earth. It is now time to be birthing elements as well.

9 𝒬𝒜

A Personal Definition of
the New Age

THERE ARE MANY WAYS OF SEEING AND INTERPRETING THE idea of the new age. It is like a diamond, possessing many facets. If we see change as brought about through science and technology, then it is that facet of the diamond which attracts us, and any other facets may be ignored or considered unimportant. The same is true if we see our power lying in political or economic—or spiritual—strategies.

Of course, the new age is all of these facets, occurring in all professions, in all walks of life, in a wide variety of situations and cultural circumstances. It is the jewel that contains them all. It organizes our efforts and experiences of change into labors of birth. However, the very vastness and variety of activities, services, products, places, teachings, and events that claim to be new age can be bewildering, especially to someone new to the idea. I find them over-whelming myself at times.

I would therefore like to offer my own definition of what the new age is. It is evolving, as I continue to explore and learn more about this spirit myself. It has an incompleteness defined by the boundaries of my own background and interests and thus serves to identify me and my biases as much as it does the characteristics of a new age.

There are four levels at which this image of the new age may be met and explored. The first is as a superficial label, usually in a commercial setting. A quick perusal of *New Age* magazine or *East West Journal,* both of which have national distribution, or of any of the many smaller new age–oriented publications will demonstrate this application: one can acquire new age shoes, wear new age clothes, use new age toothpaste, shop at new age businesses, and eat at new age restaurants where new age music is played softly in the background.

There should be no surprise that a situation like this has developed; any association that might help market a product or a service to a group of people is bound to be used to do so. As in any dealing with the marketplace, buyer discrimination is important. For myself, when something is touted as being "new age," I can almost bet that it isn't, at least not in the way I would use the term. In some cases, though, the label is quite accurate; an item is an expression of the spirit of an emerging world view or has resulted from a legitimate exploration of it. However, this spirit is usually quite capable of speaking for itself through the quality and integrity of its manifestation, without needing supportive advertising. This is the case with Paul Winter's *Missa Gaia,* to my mind a truly new age piece of music.

The second level is what I call the "new age as glamour." This is the context in which individuals and groups are living out their own fantasies of adventure and power, usually of an occult or millennarian form. Many UFO-oriented groups fall into this category.

The principal characteristic of this level is attachment to a private world of ego fulfillment and a consequent (though not always apparent) withdrawal from the world. On this level, the new age has become populated with strange and exotic beings, masters, adepts, extraterrestrials; it is a place of psychic powers and occult mysteries, of conspiracies and hidden teachings. Having encountered this world during the early days when Myrtle and I were working together in California, I can testify to its attraction for many people. It is in many ways a fun and exciting place to be, filled with enough philosophical and spiritual truths so as not to collapse entirely but heavily overlayed with distortions, wish projections, and emotional needs.

A possible and unfortunate characteristic of this level of new age thought is that the will and creativity of the individual is often surrendered to a powerful leader or a glamorous cause. This is a milieu populated with dynamic, magnetic leaders and followers who have subtly surrendered their individuality to the image of the cause, the teacher, or the group. It is the realm of the true believer, for whom the new age is a crusade and who is therefore willing both to manipulate and to be manipulated on its behalf. As a consequence, at this level we often discover the new age as an ideology, separating the faithful from the unbelievers, those who are privy to great mysteries from those who aren't, those on the side of evolution from those who would obstruct it, those who will be saved from those who won't.

It is in this context that one is most likely to find the words *new age* used, unfortunately, often by its most visible and vocal exponents. Thus, it is the source for much of the general public's awareness of the idea of a new age, which is consequently distorted. However, there is little real power for transformation in this level; aside from altering some of its terminology and coloration over the past twenty years, it has hardly changed at all.

The third level is the new age as an image of change. Here the distinguishing characteristic is the idea of transformation itself, usually expressed as a paradigm shift. A paradigm is a set of basic assumptions about something. Originally it meant the assumptions underlying a scientific hypothesis. Through wide application in a social context, the word has come to mean the assumptions and values—or world view—at the heart of a particular culture, which govern the basic direction and choices of that culture.

Our current culture is considered to be guided by the "industrial" paradigm, a set of values about work, the nature of the human being, nature, and reality as a whole that can support the existence of an industrial society. These in turn are being replaced or augmented by a new set of values, which make up the paradigm of the "postindustrial world," in effect, the new age.

This image of the new age is the one most popularly presented to the public, in books such as Willis Harman's *An Incomplete Guide to the Future*, Marilyn Ferguson's *The Aquarian Conspiracy*, and physicist Fritjof Capra's *The Turning Point*. It is the level discussed in many international and regional conferences, debated by futurists and social theorists, and explored in government projects such as the Global 2000 report to President Jimmy Carter. In this context the idea of an emerging new culture is usually seen in social, economic, and technological terms rather than spiritual ones, and the term *new age* itself is rarely used.

Much of my teaching work about emergence, particularly in the university setting, deals with this third level. However, in part due to my background, there is a final level that is even more representative to me of what the new age is truly about. This level is that of the new age as an incarnation of the sacred. Transformation is seen as the maturation of a spirit within humanity and within Gaia, maintaining continuity with the past but giving it a new fulfillment in expression.

On this level the new age is fundamentally a spiritual event, the birth of a new consciousness, a new awareness and experience of life. It is humanity becoming more fully integrated with the being of Gaia, more fully at one with the presence of God. It is a deepening into the sacramental nature of everyday life, an awakening of the consciousness that can celebrate divinity within the ordinary and, in this celebration, bring to life a sacred civilization. It is the new age as a state of being, a mode of relationship with others that is mutually empowering and enriching. Rather than spiritual *experience*, which is the focus one is more apt to find in the second level—that of psychic and spiritual glamour—this level centers upon the spiritual *function*, which is service: the giving of life, the nourishing of life, the upholding of life in its desire to unfold.

If the new age is truly the emergence of a new, holistic culture, then this fourth level is concerned with identifying, naming, and exploring the nature of the sacred experience that lies at the heart of that culture. This is not just a religious search, for the experience of the sacred is not only religious. It is also intellectual, artistic, emotional, and physical, and the naming of the sacred—the reidentification of the sacred—takes place in all these fields. Lorian, Lindisfarne, and Chinook are three new age centers that have coalesced essentially around this interpretation of the new age idea, along with the work being done at the Cathedral of St. John the Divine.

For me, with my background of mystical experiences and talking with John, this issue of "renaming the sacred" is most deeply what the new age is all about. I mean by this phrase a shift in our perception of what we recognize as the "sacred" in our lives. In our industrial culture, the rise of a materialistic world view increasingly narrowed the category of what was holy in the world, until now it is all too often confined within a closed, religious context. The sacred becomes what we encounter on whichever sabbath day we celebrate, or a being we turn to hopefully in prayer. We do not find it in changing the diapers, doing the dishes, mowing the lawn, working in a factory, programming a computer, or in any of the multitude of things we do during a day. If we did, we would give more attention and quality to them. We do not find it in nature. If we did, we would not treat the ecology of our world—the ecology that sustains us—as we do. We do not find it in each other. If we did, we would not so often treat each other as things, without regard for the holiness within us.

To rename the sacred is to have a different view of the universe. It is to reexpand those boundaries we have placed around God, even to redefine the nature of divinity, as some new theologies are doing. It is to look at the objects, people, and events in our lives and to say "You are sacred. In you and with you I can find the sacramental passages that reconnect me to the wholeness of creation." It is then to ask ourselves what kind of culture, what kind of institutions—be they political, economic, artistic, educational, or scientific—we need that can honor that universal sacredness. It is also to see the possibilities of the sacred within ourselves and to ask what kind of person we need to be to enable those institutions, that culture, that spirit to emerge in our world.

Out of all these considerations, then, I have developed the following criteria for recognizing the new age spirit at work when I encounter it:

First, it offers a positive image of the future. Equally important, it offers a vision of my capacity to create that future. It gives me a sense of what the authors of *Seven Tomorrows* call "voluntary history," the belief that "human choices can make a difference." I am not a victim of the future; I am a cocreator of its emergence, a midwife at its birth.

Second, it offers a world view to guide my choices. This world view has five primary characteristics. It is holistic, in that it affirms the interconnectedness and intercommunion of all things and the fact that the actions of any part of that wholeness affects every other part. It is therefore ecological, affirming Gaia and our role as participants in, and stewards of, the well-being of nature.

It is androgynous, affirming the unique contributions of men and women but also affirming that in our personhood we may transcend gender. The new age is neither for men's rights nor for women's rights, except temporarily where either sex may be struggling against unjust limitations; it is for the rights of persons, recognizing that maleness and femaleness are halves of a single wholeness, which can be found in each of us. However, paradoxically, it also affirms the modern need to reconnect with the image and power of the feminine insofar as that image means the essential qualities of nurturing, caring, and openness to the regenerative and vital energies of earth so necessary to the rhythm of life.

This world view is mystical, affirming, in the words of Thomas Berry, the "experience of the sacred presence within all aspects of life," including what we normally call nonlife; therefore, this world view encourages us to treat all things not only as ourselves, as the holistic view would see it, but as honored and precious manifestations of God.

This world view is global. The emergence of a planetary culture is an essential element of its perspective. Such a world culture is not the same as a world government, however. Rather, it is a state of world *communion.* It is a condition in which we share allegiance with both our native culture and nation and with our common humanity. It is the emergence of an awareness in which we dedicate ourselves in practical ways to the well-being of all persons everywhere, not just to those who live within our own national boundaries.

Finally, this world view encourages self-realization, the sanctity of the emergence of self-awareness, creativity, and accountability, within individuals and also within groups. This is not the ego self of separation but the self that lives in mutuality and finds its fulfillment not only in realizing its unique potentials but in empowering and sharing in the unfoldment of others and of society as a whole. It is also the self that does not seek only its humanness or only its transcendental nature but desires the integration of both, to their mutual empowerment, discovering and honoring the sacredness in both levels of its nature. Then, from this inner wholeness, it seeks as well its integration with the "self" of nature to discover the necessary and appropriate synthesis of person and planet.

Third, the new age offers action. These actions may be of many natures, as people identify and pursue projects that will serve their communities in ways that nourish the emergence of a new cultural vision. For me, however, the central action, which is reflected in all else we do on behalf of this vision, is the renaming of the sacred and exploring the sacraments of ordinary daily living that honor that renaming. From this act compassion flows, inspiring and guiding all the other tasks we must undertake for the healing and nourishing of each other and our world.

Fourth, as might be expected from my background, I see the new age not just as a vision but as a very real spirit. This is not a being like John but rather a presence made up of the collective spirit of humanity, and the spirit of our world, of Gaia. This spirit is reaching for a new level of beingness and creativity, a new level of integration with the earth, and a deeper state of communion with God.

PART II   Rebirth

When you go around the earth in an hour and a half, you begin to recognize that your identity is with that whole thing.

—RUSSELL SCHWEICKART

10

The Embryology of a
New Culture

How does a new culture come into being? What is its
embryology? For the idea of a new age to be more than
just a vision or an ideal it must have some way of translat-
ing itself into substance. It may be, as my friend John puts
it, a spiritual reality already, but it still needs to materialize
before human beings can experience it.

It is encouraging to think of the new age as a single coordinated movement, and the thrust of my experience has
been that there is some truth to this image, at least when
considered from a spiritual perspective. This unity, however, is not much manifest in the physical world. Marilyn
Ferguson writes that a "leaderless but powerful network is
working to bring about radical change in the United
States," and calls it the Aquarian conspiracy. This image is

more a literary device, though, than a full statement of fact, and as such can be misleading (particularly for those individuals who tend to see the threat of conspiracies everywhere, anyway). It is true, as Marilyn so ably documents in her book, that there are an increasing number of people in all walks of life and professions who are working for creative change in our society, and it is true that most of them share a similar vision of a more humane and holistic culture. Yet they are far from united. What unity there is comes from the emergence of a common *idea* rather than a common *strategy*.

When we study the Industrial Revolution, we do not confuse it with other historical revolutions, such as the revolt of the American colonials against Great Britain. We do not see it as clandestine meetings of technicians plotting the overthrow of a monarchy nor as hordes of mechanics and factory workers storming the barricades of the medieval world. We understand that it was a historical movement brought about by changes in technology and in our world view. Similarly, to think of the new age as a conspiracy or as a plot, as some religious and political groups do (encouraged, no doubt, by Marilyn Ferguson's unfortunate book title) is to indulge in misplaced concreteness and totally misconstrue the nature of what is happening. There is, as Marilyn points out, no single leader, no charismatic figure, no central group that is orchestrating the emergence of a new world view in our time. There is no master blueprint for emergence nor even any single strategy. It is the outgrowth of the thinking, feeling, exploring, aspiring, searching, creating efforts of millions of people, most of whom may never have thought in terms of building a new age. Many of these individual efforts are even in conflict with each other. Those who seek a better world but who see human nature as fundamentally flawed are going to use a different approach (usually more authoritarian and regimented) than will those who see human beings as essentially whole, sacred individuals with an innate core of lov-ingness.

Even among those who believe in the idea of a new age, strategies may differ. If I see that concept simply as a new kind of advertising label, then I may look for ways to pro-mote it as a means of gaining an economic or social advan-tage. I have met politicians who glibly talk about the new age and cultural transformation to appropriate audiences simply as a means of gaining votes, but who haven't the slightest clue as to what the spirit and values of such a new culture are really about. (If they did, they wouldn't at-tempt to be so manipulative.)

If my image of the new age is that of the paradigm shift, then I will evolve strategies to create change, or com-municate the new paradigm, or demonstrate alternative life-styles. I might, for example, concentrate on the devel-opment of techniques for using renewable energy sources, such as solar or wind power. I might start an intentional community in which certain values could be explored and demonstrated. I might develop educational programs to show how one world view is giving way to another.

On the other hand, if I see the new age as primarily a spiritual deepening or a change of consciousness, then my strategies will be more subjective. I may follow a spiritual practice, perhaps a meditative discipline. I may seek ways of implementing a more inclusive sense of the sacred in my daily life, seeing my ordinary tasks as sacraments in which, through the attitude and quality with which I do them, I may reveal a presence of holiness and wholeness.

Also, the spiritual approach to the new age is more fo-cused on deepening than on change. It has similarities to the attitude of a gardener. It seeks not so much to break with the past as to nurture the fruits of our history. It honors continuity and, without sacrificing its vision of new possibilities and revelations, seeks connectedness with the soil of tradition. As well as developing new images, and engaging in projects that give form to a new cultural vision, the spiritual approach will also highlight what is best in the old culture and work for metamorphosis from within.

At one time or another, I may use many of these approaches or combinations of them. I may become involved in medical strategies such as the holistic healing movement, political strategies such as supporting candidates who embody holistic values (or being such a candidate myself), economic strategies such as voluntary simplicity or developing more democratic and synergistic labor and management relationships and practices, or educational strategies, such as designing new ways of learning and of enhancing the creativity and mutuality of children and adults.

There are many possibilities, and there are a number of books and publications on the market exploring the potential strategies for emergence, among the best of which are *The Little Green Book,* by John Lobell, and *Networking,* by Jessica Lipnack and Jeffrey Stamps. Whatever strategies I choose for learning and acting, they should, of course, reflect my individual interests, skills, and talents and the needs or characteristics of my environment; it is better for me to do what I can do best in the moment (and perhaps learn to do more later) and what is in harmony with my nature than to attempt to follow someone else's master blueprint or an idealized, abstract strategy presented in a book. For me, one of the empowering aspects about this process of emergence is that we must find *our own* way into it and discover for ourselves what our best contributions may be. In other words, one of the key strategies is our own process of unfoldment and self-discovery.

I do not wish to give an impression, however, that the "Aquarian" unfoldment is totally haphazard and amorphous. It is, as Marilyn Ferguson, Willis Harman, Fritjof Capra, economist Hazel Henderson, and others have been pointing out, defined by an increasingly clear set of ideas

and values: the content of the new paradigm. This content
influences the nature and direction of each strategy. Further, there is a clear convergence of individuals, groups,
and organizations going on around these values, creating
an emerging network that in fact is beginning to act in
more concerted and coordinated ways. Strategies are also
determined by the embryology of the new culture, the
needs it must fulfill if it is to become real.

A new culture emerges in four stages, on both the individual level and the level of society. The first is self-discovery. The second is self-development. Integration with
the environment and with history is the third, while the
fourth is service, that is, the work that leads to a meaningful existence.

Self-discovery, the first stage, is most important. All cultures are outgrowths of implicitly held ideas, values, and
images concerning the nature of reality and the role of humanity within it. When a new culture seeks to emerge, it
must take time to identify and clarify what its implicit assumptions—its paradigm—may be. To fail to do this is to
risk simply adopting and adapting the older paradigm, giving it quick cosmetic changes perhaps, but basically taking
it over relatively intact. The power of habit and inertia, the
subtle tyranny of the familiar, insures that this would happen if efforts were not made to avoid it.

During this first stage, therefore, the strategies are those
of challenge, investigation, and exploration. There is a need
to challenge the older assumptions and gain some distance
from them. There is the need to try out new values, to see
what works and what doesn't. There can be a lot of pain
during this stage, a lot of false starts and wrong turnings.
There can be an unnecessary degree of separation with
what has gone before and energy wasted in "reinventing
the wheel."

A good example of this on individual levels is the desire
for independence of older children and adolescents. I can

well remember telling my father not to show me how to do something, that I wanted to learn to do it for myself. That the task might take longer or that I might not do as good a job was not the point, since the real object of the exercise was to discover my own abilities.

Sometimes in groups as well as in individuals the desire for self-discovery takes the form of rebellion against tradition and authority. Up to a point this can be expected and useful, but rebellion itself can become the new form. When this happens, vision can be lost in a mindless flailing about at what we don't like.

A counterculture is a first step toward self-discovery, but it is not an image of the future. To do things simply because they are different or "alternative" to the way things are done in the currently dominant culture is not to assist emergence; it is to pursue novelty for its own sake. That kind of behavior can hinder the process of emergence by denying to it the power of continuity. There is much that humanity has gained in its history that should not be discarded simply because it is old or traditional. The new culture will share many values and practices with the older one; it does, however, need to discern where that sharing can best take place and where new ground needs to be broken.

A culture is like a living organism. During this first stage it is like a baby, and its strategies are similarly self-oriented. These are not strategies for helping or working within the dominant culture, any more than a baby takes on activities designed to help a family pay its bills. As the spirit of the new seeks to discover itself, it is not obligated to take on the challenges and problems of the older society. The young culture must discover its own strengths and approaches, not have its creative energy coopted or coerced into addressing the problems in old ways simply in order to satisfy a sense of "doing the right thing" as understood by the failing culture itself.

During the years I lived at Findhorn, we were often confronted by visitors who wanted to know what the community was doing on behalf of the world's starving or the peace movement, or any number of other worthy causes. Why were we living stuck away in northern Scotland, away from the hurly-burly of the modern world? Where was our relevance? What such individuals failed to realize was that Findhorn in its early days was more like a social and spiritual research laboratory than a service center; it was a place where certain ideas and values could be explored and tried out before being released to the public, so to speak. Its relative isolation was necessary to its job, for its work was to nurture a new vision in a setting where it would not be repressed.

One of the pitfalls of this stage that I have observed is that of groups or individuals taking action or creating something without a clear understanding of the essential values involved. This usually happens when a person or an organization is impatient to "do something," to "make a difference," to "stop talking and start acting," to be "relevant." It comes from an awkwardness with the "baby" stage and its particular limitations and demands and from a desire to be an "adult" immediately. Unfortunately, in such situations, the vision and understanding of the new does not have a chance to clarify itself. The actions end up reflecting old habits, taking on the *appearance* of being new age without expressing the spirit.

An example of this is a now-defunct therapeutic organization in California. Its literature and its classes all espoused ideals of individual creativity, wholeness, and freedom, and claimed that its purpose was to empower people. In the beginning, it made serious efforts toward accomplishing these ideals. However, in the interest of protecting what it saw as the purity of its spiritual qualities—a purity necessary, its leaders believed, in order to be truly new age—the organization became increasingly hierarchical and repressive. Rather than empowering individuals, it began disempowering and controlling them, even to the point of telling some people that they had to leave their husbands or wives because the spouses had become "agents of dark forces"—which in most cases simply meant they disagreed with the policies and methods of the group leaders. All the old trappings of personal and organizational power struggles appeared, leading to the sorry dichotomy of an organization preaching self-development and freedom but practicing in its own ranks repression and conformity. Eventually, this group fell apart due to its internal contradictions between vision and practice.

Avoiding such contradictions is a necessity for new age groups that expect to be integrated and effective agents for transformation. There are times in the lives of every organism when it is supposed to think, not act, reflect, not leap ahead. It is supposed to see where it is going, so that it later won't have to undo actions performed in haste and without a sense of direction. It is essential that groups give themselves the time and the permission to be temporarily irrelevant to the larger society if necessary in order to gain this clarity of vision. Their relevance will then come from service based on this clarity. In the years since I was there, Findhorn has been a source of inspiration to people that has encouraged a great deal of creative action on behalf of many causes. It has expanded itself to incorporate new elements, such as experiments in appropriate technology, that it could not have undertaken in the early years. Those early years, however, provide the foundation for the growing relevancy of its services.

The second stage is *self-development*, building a body of expression that honors and accurately reflects the vision at the center. Strategies at this stage include discernment (knowing what expressions should be kept from the exploratory days and what should be discarded); a discipline of implementation, organization, and demonstration;

greater public outreach (usually through educational or artistic programs); and, very important, networking. The objective is to build an infrastructure of connections and links, shared resources and projects, through which the spirit and forms of a new culture can begin to materialize.

The Chinook Learning Community is a good example of this stage in action. The community began as little more than a single family living on a farm in the woods, exploring what the vision of a new age meant to them. It gradually grew to include a few others, rarely more than half a dozen, who continued and expanded the process of reflection and learning. In time they began sponsoring classes and retreats. After about five years of this preparatory work, they began a program of public outreach, which now includes an extensive educational program, a developing ecological village, and small businesses. They have also entered into a growing network of association and shared endeavors with similar groups both locally and in other parts of the United States. They are also beginning to work more closely with mainstream organizations, such as churches, schools, and businesses in their area, and are in the process of developing and supporting public service projects around Seattle that will not be identified with Chinook alone or even directly.

This latter step on Chinook's part represents the third stage in the unfoldment of a new age group: *the integration with history and with the larger environment*. During the first two stages, the cultural organism that is emerging and the groups that embody it are generally characterized by self-involvement, often in conflict with the older society. In the third stage a deeper sense of accountability takes over. The idea of two cultures gives way to a more transcendent realization of one human spirit seeking to develop on one planet. The emerging culture must now integrate with its world. It must discover its links with the existing cultures and with history. It must discover how it can be an agent of continuity as much as of transformation, and how it can be a source of fulfillment for the best that is in the old society, even as it seeks to replace what isn't working. The counterculture must give way to the *communion culture*.

A number of new age groups are at this stage, reaching out to traditional institutions like the university or the church, business and politics, even into the military, in order to develop a creative interface. At that point of meeting, distinctions like "old age" and "new age" fall away. Individuals try to pool their talents and visions to give birth to a human society that works with greater harmony and nourishment for all life.

Out of this arises the true new culture, the synthesis of a new paradigm with the wisdom and roots of what has gone before, ready to take its place as a responsible member of a world community. This stage is still in its infancy. Most individuals and groups interested in a new age are still too focused upon transformation and the appearance of new forms to see the value in what already is or has been and to form appropriate links with history and with the larger culture.

There is a frequent image that one encounters among "new paradigm groups." This is the image of the "quantum leap," the idea that the transformation can come suddenly because of the development of a critical mass of people believing in and practicing the values and strategies of the new paradigm. Then, the influence of this critical mass upon the collective unconscious of humanity will bring a new consciousness and a new social model into existence within a very short span of time, practically overnight as historical processes go.

There is some evidence from science that such spontaneous transformations can occur, and there is no question, as I have already discussed, but that the pace of change in our world has greatly accelerated during the century. On the other hand, this idea of the quantum leap (an image taken from quantum mechanics, in which a unit of energy can move instantaneously from one energy state to another without any intervening steps) as believed in and taught by some new age writers comes very close in tone to the older image of apocalypse. This is not because it projects images of disaster but because it envisions an appearance of the new culture without the necessary process of work and integration to bring it about. It takes on magical overtones. In a peculiar spiraling back to attitudes of the early sixties, people are simply waiting for this quantum leap that will make the world right again.

Paradoxically, one of the greater drawbacks to the emergence of a new culture is the idea of the new age itself. It can keep us from moving from the third to the fourth stage. We focus upon the images of change and transformation and forget to give attention to that which is emerging. Is it possible to embody it now? If so, what do we need to do? As I mentioned, these were the questions that Findhorn confronted in 1970, when it decided it would be the new culture now, not in any final form but attempting to embody new values. A quantum leap may well occur in human consciousness and outlook, but not by trying to make it happen. It would come about by going beyond it, by assuming it has already taken place, by getting down to the practical business of expressing a new cultural vision in the midst of ordinary, everyday personal and planetary problems.

The fourth stage, then, is *the embodiment of new values in service*. At this stage, people recognize that even if there is a spontaneous transformation in human consciousness, there is still a need to integrate it with the world we now experience. I may have a sudden change of mind, but it doesn't mean my physical world suddenly rearranges itself accordingly. I have to act out of my new perspective and translate it into new behavior.

It is naïve to imagine that all the cultures of the world

will spontaneously become productive members of a planetary community. Humanity is not monolithic; it exists in too many different states of being and consciousness. A new cultural spirit may indeed become swiftly dominant, but there will still be work to do to implement and integrate it into our history.

The fourth stage arrives when an individual or group has gained an inner strength of vision and creativity—a maturity of spirit. They can then take the long view of history and settle down for an extended process of service and work. Such a mature spirit does not expect nor need the instant gratification of experiencing its vision (and version) of a new world immediately. It understands that the energy of emergence, the whole new age idea is only a means, not a goal, that one cannot continue to live in an attitude of Aquarian "conspiracy" if one hopes to live in Aquarius itself. The idea of transformation is a catalyst, not the final product, and its fate will be to disappear into a greater synthesis between past, present, and future, old culture and new, that will in fact create the reality ahead, the sacred civilization yearned for by both the human spirit and the rest of the living world.

11

Images to Live By

WHEN I FIRST HEARD OF THE NEW AGE IN 1959, I WAS NOT familiar with the concept of a paradigm, much less a paradigm shift. Although used widely by grammarians and biblical scholars, the term *paradigm* did not come into its current usage until after 1962, when Thomas Kuhn used it in *The Structure of Scientific Revolutions* to mean a fundamental model of an accepted idea. The idea of an emerging culture based on a new world view was generally not part of the context of the new age idea in those days. The new age was defined by apocalypse and transformation, not by paradigms and cultures.

Once the term caught on it became so overused that by the late seventies it had begun to take on the character of a buzz word, part of a new jargon. One reason for its wide-

spread use was that it provided a way to talk about some
very real changes in perception and understanding that
were occurring during the past twenty years. The paradigm
shift became a legitimate and accurate way to talk about
transformation. By contrast, the generally esoteric and
apocalyptic language and images of the new age milieu
were often too restricted and "otherworldly."

Furthermore, the idea of a paradigm shift leads to strategies and actions. Transformation becomes as accessible as
a change of mind. With an apocalyptic view, as I mentioned before, all one can do is hunker down and wait. It
has always seemed to me a paradoxical failure of imagination on the part of many new age groups of the late fifties
and early sixties that while they could weave the most fan-
tastic scenarios of earthquakes, polar shifts, the tilting of
the earth on its axis, visitations from flying saucers, and
various supernatural happenings, they could not imagine
transformation brought about by thousands of people
learning to see themselves and their planet differently. This
assumption of powerlessness and helplessness on the part
of humanity has always been a failing of the apocalyptic
viewpoint.

The literature of the paradigm shift is large and growing,
so much so, in fact, that some of its terms are in danger of
becoming meaningless. This, I feel, is the case with the
term *holistic*, a central image in the new paradigm. Like
the new age, this word is widely used now as a come-on, an
advertising slogan or gimmick which, when attached to certain products or practices, is supposed to impute a special
quality. It becomes an indication of trendiness, not of
transformation.

I do not want to add to this condition by belaboring the
issue of the new paradigm. Its message, in essence, is an
ecological one—to live with awareness in a universe that is
interconnected and interdependent, in which the well-being of each part is the responsibility of every other part be-

cause ultimately all are part of one being. Jesus and other great models of humanity say it simply: to love God, to love oneself, and to love one's neighbor. Holism is simply another way to talk about love in action.

What makes this paradigm new is its connection with and, to some extent, derivation from the work being done in science, such as in ecology but particularly in physics. So revolutionary, by modern materialistic standards, is the view of reality emerging from the study of energy and subatomic realms that it challenges most of the assumptions on which our culture is based.

Our society has long believed in the primacy of matter (at any rate, we act as if we do, even when we profess a belief in spirit), in the separation of mind and body, in the separation and isolation of material objects from each other, and in a universe where life may be an accident but where, at any rate, it develops and evolves through random mutations and laws of competition that favor the strongest and fittest.

According to the latest findings in physics, ecology, medicine, zoology, bacteriology, and chemistry, none of these assumptions are true. We remain in the grip of nineteenth century thinking, believing in a universe that doesn't exist. The basic message of the new paradigm is that far from living in "the real world," as pragmatists so love to call it, we are living in an imaginary world that through its distortions might well kill us all unless we wake up to reality.

For example, according to David Bohm, a physicist whose work in subatomic physics has had a strong influence on the development of the new paradigm, "The true state of affairs in the material world is wholeness. If we are fragmented, we must blame it on ourselves." This quote is from an interview with Bohm in *The Holographic Paradigm and Other Paradoxes*, edited by Ken Wilber. Bohm goes on to say,

Relativity and, even more important, quantum mechanics have strongly suggested (though not proved) that the world cannot be analyzed into separate and independently existing parts. Moreover, each part somehow involves all the others: contains them or enfolds them. This fact suggests that the sphere of ordinary material life and the sphere of mystical experience have a certain shared order and that this will allow a fruitful relationship between them.

What Bohm and other quantum physicists are saying is that matter is not a thing at all but an event; it is a process existing within something else, an unbroken wholeness which Bohm has called the "that-which-is," or the "implicate order." Within this domain of unity, everything is in touch somehow with everything else, everything interconnected and interrelated. This is the kind of universe I experienced when I was seven years old, and it is the traditional mystical view of reality.

Other scientists in other disciplines have added to this world view. Neurophysiologist Karl Pribram has proposed through his studies on memory and brain functions that the brain has the capacity to tune into a realm, similar to Bohm's implicate order, in which all the information in creation is evenly distributed and therefore universally available. Because this realm has characteristics similar to a hologram, a three-dimensional photograph, Pribram's theory is called the holographic paradigm. It is, by the way, one of the first scientific theories that provides a model to explain psychic phenomena.

The implication of these and other theories is that the phenomena we know as life and consciousness may be the true substance of creation, the primal energy or implicate order from which everything derives. This means that both these qualities are not isolated phenomena but everywhere present. It also means that at some level, through our own

lives and consciousnesses, we participate in cocreating the
world we experience. We are part of the creative process.
To exist is to participate, and to participate is to create.
This is a far cry from the view of humanity as a powerless
accident at the mercy of a dead universe.

I have already discussed the Gaia hypothesis that the
earth is a living being. One of the developers of that hypothesis, Dr. Lynn Margulis, is a microbiologist who has
done pioneering research into the origin of the eukaryotic
cell. This is the cell with a nucleus, such as those that make
up our own bodies. Her work in this area has shown that
the nucleated cell is really a community of smaller organisms, living and working together in symbiosis. Indeed, her
research suggests strongly that symbiosis is as important a
force in evolution as competition, and that evolutionary
success may even be more likely to go to the most cooperative than to the strongest.

An even more radical theory of evolution was recently
developed by an English biochemist and plant physiologist,
Dr. Rupert Sheldrake. In *A New Science of Life* he offers
evidence in support of the existence of what he calls morphogenetic fields. These are fields of connection between
all the members of a particular species, fields as yet unrecognized by modern physics but perhaps existing in a manner related to Bohm's implicate order. Through a process of
"morphic resonance," organisms can "tune in" to the behavior and experience of other members of the species, both
those presently alive and those who have gone before (the
pattern of their behavior being recorded in the field itself). It can then modify its own behavior based on the information contained in the morphogenetic field. For example, when an animal has learned a certain type of behavior,
other animals of the same species anywhere in the world
have a simpler time learning the same thing.

This has tremendous implications for the transmission of
knowledge and behavior. It and other similar theories com-

ing out of the fields of chemistry and biology suggest that a cultural transformation and the adoption of a new paradigm could come about very swiftly—out of the learning and embodiment of the essentials of that new vision by only a few members of our species.

The images emerging out of science have similar characteristics and implications. They all indicate the holistic nature of the universe. They also all indicate the power and influence of each part of that universe: no single individual is too unimportant to be able to make a contribution. From this flows other values of the new paradigm: its humanistic orientation, its commitment to ecology, its encouragement of a transcendental world view, its support of community and the arts of connectedness and ways of empowering the individual, such as greater decentralization in the political and economic realms.

Two common misunderstandings about this new paradigm should be emphasized. The first concerns the role of science. Ever since Fritjof Capra wrote his landmark book, *The Tao of Physics,* in the middle of the seventies, in which he demonstrated the similarities between the emerging holistic world view of physics and the world view of eastern and western mysticism, there has been a tendency to say that science is now "proving" mysticism (although Capra himself has never made that claim). It is more precise to say that mysticism and science are converging and that both point to a universe whose nature transcends them both.

I consider myself to have a foot in both camps. Though most of my life has been spent on what some would call a mystical path, my early professional background is in science. For me there has never been a conflict between them, even in college when I would study genetics and chemistry during the day and meditate at night. Science and mysticism both represent ways of knowing about reality. Each has its strengths, each its limitations.

This emerging understanding can be muddled when new age and mystically oriented people take up new scientific theories, such as the right-brain, left-brain discoveries or, more recently, Pribram's holographic theory, and make them a foundation on which to support and legitimatize various psychic and transcendental notions about reality. Mysticism does not need to be proved by science, nor vice versa. To attempt to do so often is to end up with bad science and bad mysticism. However, the mystic can and should make use of the clarity and precision of the scientific method, as far as it will go in that domain, and the scientist can well make use of the intuition and deeper insights that mystical training can provide. In short, they can be complements to each other, but we should avoid making them fit into each other's shoes.

A second danger is that of applying the new paradigm in a nonholistic way. Often it is contrasted with the older, mechanistic paradigm, which appears to emphasize values of competition, exploitation, profit, centralization, and unlimited material growth at the expense of the environment. We should remember that industrial civilization has brought us many benefits, and that the mechanistic paradigm that supports it is not unrelievedly ugly. Both cultural views share values in common. Nor is the new paradigm absolutely pure and right. It will have its shadows, too. One can already see them in the form of groups that in the name of wholeness trample on individual rights, or individuals who, in the name of self-realization and growth, conveniently forget their accountability to others.

If we are pilgrims en route to a holistic civilization, then we need to remember that this is a process which must reflect its destination at all points. As Krishnamurti has said, "The first step is the last." We cannot pay lip service to a paradigm of wholeness but not embody it until the new world is all around us. We cannot use it as a source of division against the culture in which we now live. At some

point, if the new paradigm is true and resonates with the
deepest needs in humanity, as well as with the real nature
of the universe, then it will succeed, and we will then find
ourselves responsible for the world as it is. It is always
easier to be a revolutionary than to be an administrator. If
the new paradigm is true in its insights, we are already the
administrators, and we need to act accordingly, even toward those parts of the world that seem in opposition to us.
To engage in a battle of the paradigms is to miss the point.
It is to deny wholeness in the name of wholeness.

12

A Preview

THE IDEA OF A NEW AGE AS AN IMAGE OF THE FUTURE OFFERS us several things. It provides us an alternative to images of pessimism and despair. It maintains that the future need not be determined by inertia, habit, or the momentum of the present—transformation is possible. By challenging current cultural assumptions about ourselves and our world, this idea encourages revisioning and innovative thinking. Further, it offers us a new set of values, a new world view to guide our efforts at future-building.

Predicting the future is a modern growth industry. In magazines like *The Futurist*, published by the World Future Society, and in books like Alvin Toffler's *The Third Wave*, Hazel Henderson's *Creating Alternative Futures*, or *Resettling America*, edited by Gary Coates, writers seek to

put flesh on the forms through which the new world view
might embody itself. In some cases these forms are already
visible. In *Networking*, Jessica Lipnack and Jeffrey Stamps
talk about an expression of a new culture already amongst
us and functioning: "The networking that creates the universe we call Another America." Calling this new culture
"not a place but a state of mind," they write:

> Touching every area of our lives, there is Another
> America, not often seen on television or read about in
> newspapers. It is an Emerald City of ideas and visions
> and practical enterprises that people move in and out of
> depending on their moods and needs, a domain that is
> very new, and at the same time, very old.
>
> In this special universe, health is perceived as the nat-
> ural state of the body, cooperation is regarded as an
> effective way to meet basic needs, nature's ecological or-
> chestra is revered as one unified instrument, inner devel-
> opment is valued as a correlate to social involvement,
> and the planet is understood to be an interconnected
> whole.

In a similar vein, social forecaster John Naisbitt writes in
his book *Megatrends* of ten major trends in modern society
that already manifest the qualities of a new culture. Among
these are shifts from an industrial-based economy to one
based on the development and distribution of information;
from a national economy to a global one; from economic
and political centralization to greater decentralization and
local self-reliance; and from hierarchical models of organization to the more dynamic and holistic model of the network.

A detailed blueprint, however, while giving us clear direction, can also limit our innovative and creative alertness.
It can fix our attention upon a particular way of doing
things, a particular goal or plan, and reduce our willingness

or capacity to perceive new options and change our direction if necessary. It is wise to remember that many great changes in history were the result of the appearance of unexpected events, discoveries, or personalities. A certain flexibility to take such unpredictabilities into account is important.

In his communications, John has spoken directly to this point. When asked by a questioner to prophesy what was ahead for humanity and what the new culture might look like, he said:

It is not our intent to offer you a blueprint. You do not need a spiritual force to tell you what is wrong in your world nor what you need to do. You already have what you require. You can see for yourselves what is amiss in your world, where suffering exists, where imbalance threatens you and other lives. You know the qualities and actions that can bring healing. You are not forsaken by God but are embraced by divinity's loving presence. Thus, you have the spirit of the Beloved on which to draw. The new age represents a challenge to the emergence of your maturity as a species. It asks if you can find in yourself the wisdom, the courage, the attunement to God, and the willingness to act on behalf of the planetary whole, that will mark you as adult in your consciousness and rational in your understanding of reality. Give your attention to healing your world as you now find it, and the future will unfold itself automatically.

Without trying to construct a blueprint or detailed prophecy, one can discern the profile of an emerging culture. First of all, we are likely to see the *integration of a planetary culture with regional cultures*. Both will be seen as necessary, and no attempt will be made to foster one at the expense of the other. Instead, each region or nation will be encouraged to contribute its own unique richness to the human experience, and diversity will be treasured as an ecological and evolutionary necessity. By the same token, equal efforts will be made to identify and nourish those qualities and connections which humanity shares in common, so that a transregional, transnational identity may emerge as well.

A *world agency* of some description will exist that can coordinate planetary networks and service agencies that deal with global issues. It will provide a focus through which the identity and will of humanity as a whole can be seen and experienced. Its function may not be recognized as governmental by today's terms but its purpose will be to synthesize efforts to deal with those problems and opportunities that cannot be handled by a single nation, such as global pollution, world hunger, perhaps even space exploration. The embryo of such an agency already exists in the United Nations and in the work of its specialized groups. On the other hand, much of the actual power and regulatory functions that we now ascribe to governments will have devolved upon regional and local bodies, providing a forum for greater citizen participation in decisions dealing with local and regional problems and issues.

"Thinking Globally and Acting Locally" (as the title of a 1981 World Future Society conference put it) will be the motto of this culture. To implement it will require that much energy and attention be put to *communication*. This would include both technological expertise and development, and the enhancement of intercultural and interpersonal understanding. The sense of communion and community will be seen as vital to good communication; the most sophisticated telephone and television system is only as good as the quality of the information that passes over it. Thus, it will be a society that places stress upon multicultural education, beginning with childhood and never stopping. It will also honor nonverbal means of communication, finding in the arts such as dance, music, and drama, skills

and techniques that greatly enhance the experience of a
planetary language. The mystical arts of meditation, intuition, and even extrasensory perception may also be
brought into play here.

Education will be seen as a lifelong process. This will be
especially true with changing images of work. With increasing automation, fewer and fewer people will be able
to provide essential goods and services for the many. Simple, linear material expansion will also be seen as wasteful
and destructive within the finite limits of the earth's biosphere, which will also bring a shift in the high consump-
tion and high waste ethic of the old industrial economy.
Many jobs and skills that were essential to that economy
will become unnecessary. However, the cultivation of our
human resources will become a new frontier, and the meaning of employment may well become synonymous with the
values of self-development and education.

Parallel and complementary to a continuing but largely
automated industrial and electronics sector may well develop *an economy based on the individual's creativity and
production.* Crafts, skills, information, and contributions to
the beauty and spiritual well-being of society will be highly
valued. While cities will continue to exist as large centers of
culture and activity, such an individualized economy may
well be based in a setting of smaller towns and villages,
where a more personal and intimate contact between a person, his or her work, the environment, and the community
can be experienced and nourished. Such villages will depend strongly on the use of renewable resources and techniques of environmental and solar architecture pioneered
by the New Alchemy Institute and similar groups. In such
a setting, a person's contribution becomes less abstract,
more direct and concrete. It can be measured in services
provided and in the quality which that person's life adds to
the community as a whole, thus providing a basis for a

wider definition of work and production than that provided simply by an economics based on monetary exchange.

Larger economic entities, akin to our corporations of today, will also exist. They will be recognized as villages and cultures in themselves, often transnational in scope and character, and will consequently have an accountability to society as a whole that transcends the economic sphere. These corporate entities will represent one of the forms through which humanity explores its collective consciousness and its capacity to create community. By virtue of being multinational, they will be important participants in the development of a planetary awareness and sensibility. Thus, they will be expected to contribute not just goods or services but a cultural identity as well and will have the same responsibilities for integration with the environment and with the planetary community as any other human grouping. Unlike the feudal systems that currently exist in many modern corporations, these new entities will be more participatory and democratic, in keeping with a general trend toward supporting individual development. However, they will also be social laboratories in which a wide variety of governmental, community, cooperative, and economic models may be experimented with.

There will be several religions and spiritual disciplines as there are today, each serving different sensibilities and affinities, each enriched by and enriching the particular cultural soil in which it is rooted. However, there will also be a *planetary spirituality* that will celebrate the sacredness of the whole of humanity in appropriate festivals, rituals, and sacraments. There will be a more widespread understanding and experience of the holistic nature of reality, resulting in a shared outlook that today would be called mystical. Mysticism has always overflowed the bounds of particular religious traditions, and in the new world this would be even more true. The observance of the sacred (or of the whole) in one's everyday life and activities would not be seen as religious but as right and normal living.

The *healing arts* will draw both on the technology of medicine as we now know it and the practice of intervention, and on the patient's own skill and understanding in taking charge of his or her own health care. The doctor will be less the authoritative expert who takes over and more the one who empowers the individual's own expertise. People will be trained from childhood in principles of diet, mind, and body integration, and self-care that will allow them, with minimal assistance from a professional, to create their own state of health, drawing on a doctor's services primarily in time of emergency or for periodic checkups and health care "refresher" courses. Indeed, this trend toward greater personal self-sufficiency will be evident in many activities. For instance, an unhealthy dependency on an over-specialized labor force may be recognized as disempowering both for a vital economy and for the individual's own sense of self-worth and creative accountability.

Along with a commitment to individual growth, there will be commitment to the *arts of mutuality*, based on the holistic insight that relationship is the essential force of creation. Whether in the context of the family, the community, the workplace, the nation, or the world, interpersonal or intraspecies skills will be honored, taught, and developed. The art of skilled and loving accountability will be an essential ingredient of society.

A new spirit of androgyny will be present, one that honors the essential person, man or woman, and also recognizes the feminine in each man, the masculine in each woman. There will be gender-specific functions and activities that will serve the uniqueness of each sex, but there will be even more activities that serve the wholeness of the person. For a culture based on a patriarchial outlook, this spirit of androgyny will come through a reconnection with the power and nature of the feminine, dealing in new and more open ways with the forces of the unconscious and of "Mother" Earth. The feminine consciousness is profoundly ecological, thus a deeper acceptance and attunement to its qualities leads to a realization of the uniqueness and common destiny of humanity and the nonhuman world. In a world perceived as a product of intercommunion between all life, no person or creature will be exploited on the basis of race, gender, or nonhumanness.

There will continue to be basic scientific research, but the holistic world view, with its insights into the universal nature of consciousness, will result in *a deeper integration between science and mysticism, technology and ecology*. In addition to traditional instrumentation and methods of experimentation, there will be added the intuitive capacities of the human mind and soul and its ability to gain information in altered states of consciousness through attunement to the "implicate order." Technology will not be seen as being intrinsically antihumanistic, as is often the case today. It will be recognized as being a very human expression, capable, like any other human activity, earthly or mystical, of being carried to extremes, but also capable of being a vessel for unfoldment and creativity. We will learn to see, in the new culture, the beauty in technology and the manner in which engineering can be a spiritual path.

This new world will not be without conflict or struggle. It may well have its blind side, and therefore, its reformers and its dissidents. The new culture is not a utopia but a different set of perceptions of the value and nature of human life. It will have its own kinds of conflicts, but it will learn to solve them without threatening extinction to all life in the process.

These are broad brush strokes of what a world based on the new paradigm might be like, leaving much more out than it puts in. If we wish the details, it is up to us now to create them, in our lives, in our society, in our world.

13

Pioneers

ONE OF THE MOST BEAUTIFUL AREAS IN THE WORLD IS THE
Puget Sound region in the Pacific Northwest. Here, a short
half-hour drive or so north of Seattle, one finds Whidbey
Island, surrounded by the Olympic mountains to the west,
the Cascade Range to the east, Mount Baker to the north,
and Mount Rainier to the south. To get to the island is a
fifteen-minute ferry ride, during which time, if you're
lucky and the season is right, you may see the beautiful
orcas, or killer whales, swimming through the channel, or
dolphins frolicking alongside the boat.

Here on south Whidbey one finds the Chinook Learning
Community, nestled in a beautiful evergreen forest and
meadowlands. Chinook is a new age center, started by a
Presbyterian minister, Fritz Hull, and his wife Vivienne.

Specifically, it is an educational center, offering programs—some lasting a year, others only for a weekend—which provide as complete and balanced an introduction to the new world view, its history, values, and implications, as well as to practical strategies for its implementation, as any I have seen anywhere.

It has a small residential community of less than a dozen people, but is the center of a growing village of supporters and coworkers, whose use of the surrounding forestland is governed by an ecologically oriented land covenant. Drawing mainly but not exclusively upon the Christian tradition (particularly Celtic Christianity, which has a strong ecological bias), it explores what might be called the theology of the new age, and runs a successful and active program for clergy of all denominations. It draws a wide range of speakers and cultural events to the Seattle area (including a special performance of Paul Winter's *Missa Gaia*) and cooperates with a number of other local groups in projects of service to the larger urban community.

Groups and centers like Chinook represent one of the principal strategies of emergence. They are like colonies of the future, laboratories in which the spirit of a new culture can discover its appropriate shapes, and like any laboratory or colony, they have their share of failures as well as successes. In the best of their work, they can provide us with previews of a possible future. What are these groups like and who are the people who create them?

Many of them, like Chinook, are educational centers. This is logical, since at this stage much of the work is that of communicating the new paradigm. Some are residential and some are not. One of the most successful of the nonresidential ones with which I am familiar is Interface in Boston, which offers a master's degree program in holistic education, including a counselor training program.

Other such groups may develop around an interest in ecology and alternative technology. The New Alchemy Institute is one example; another is a group in Wisconsin, the High Wind Association. Started by a university professor and his wife, Belden and Lisa Paulson, this organization received a small grant from the U.S. Department of Energy to build a bioshelter as a demonstration project. However, Belden's work and that of High Wind has also been very involved with education, cosponsoring a number of classes on issues of cultural transformation and the new paradigm with the University of Wisconsin, as well as offering, along with the Lorian Association, an annual intensive summer school at High Wind's small residential community.

Belden, Lisa, and High Wind are examples of people and groups associated with the idea of a new age who also maintain close links with established cultural institutions, such as the university. They seek to assist a natural process of transformation and unfoldment from within the mainstream as well as demonstrating possible alternatives from outside it.

Along the "Aquarian Frontier," as cultural historian Theodore Roszak calls it in *Unfinished Animal*, there are a number of religious groups, most of them followers of eastern teachers and gurus. These provide new spiritual insights and practices to their followers and in their own way contribute to a cultural change, if only by widening our own religious and cultural perspectives. However, in my experience, many of these are not new age in their outlook. Their work is more to foster the growth of their own religious path and to assist individuals in finding inner fulfillment (a legitimate enough motive—Christianity has been similarly proselytising and conducting missionary projects in the East for centuries). They do not necessarily embody nor express a vision of a pluralistic planetary culture.

There are exceptions to this, and one of them is the Sufi Order in the West, headed by Pir Vilayat Inayat Khan. He has been at the forefront in drawing together leading spiritual teachers of many traditions and leading scientists such as David Bohm and Karl Pribram to explore the growing convergence between science and mysticism. He and the Sufis in general have also worked diligently to create a deeper sense of unity between different world religions and spiritual practices in the interest of discovering a planetary spirituality. A person can be a Sufi and belong to any other religion, for to be a Sufi is to seek and serve the universality within humanity, not to be set apart but to nourish the mystical wholeness of our species and our planet.

Another example of the new age philosophy in action is the Lindisfarne Association, founded by William Irwin Thompson. In some ways, Lindisfarne is more a strategy than a group or a place, though it has its own small publishing firm headquartered in the Berkshires of Massachusetts and a retreat center in the mountains of southeastern Colorado, where summer classes and conferences are held. Bill, more than any other person I know, directly addresses, both in his writings and in the gatherings he sponsors, the central issues of what makes up an emerging culture. In his vision—as well as in the educational work of Lindisfarne—art, politics, science, architecture, ecology, economics, and spirituality are all synthesized, their connections revealed and discussed, their essential sacredness highlighted. The programs Lindisfarne offers are not for the idly curious or the timid; they offer and demand an intellectual rigor and a celebration of scholarship that is rare in my experience among new age groups, and an interdisciplinary outlook that is equally rare in universities.

A cornerstone of Lindisfarne's work is the association of physicists, artists, philosophers, clergy, engineers, economists, mystics, chemists, biologists, historians, architects and poets known as the Lindisfarne Fellows. Each member of the Fellows is outstanding in his or her own field, a pioneer in exploring the edges of a new culture while the fellowship itself mirrors a shared vision of the synthesis and wholeness of knowledge. The potentials for cross-fertilization between them are obvious, and some of them do work together on joint projects (a number of Fellows were involved in the completion of the *Missa Gaia*). Most, though, see each other only once a year at the annual gatherings. Still, they have an enhancing effect upon each other's work, while all represent a resource upon which Lindisfarne can draw for its educational programs.

There are new age groups that put their values into practical service to their communities, just as other charitable and service organizations do. The Farm, a very large community in Tennessee, for example, has sent out expeditions with food, medical supplies, and skilled labor to help out devastated towns and villages in Central America after a series of earthquakes in that region. The Earth Community, a new age group affiliated with the Cathedral of St. John the Divine, in New York City, organizes and sponsors food gathering and distribution for the needy of that city, as well as exploring long-range solutions to that problem through developing neighborhood solar greenhouses and block gardens.

The cathedral itself, as I have previously mentioned, is, to me, an example of a new age center in the best sense of the word. It reaches back into its tradition of cathedral building by having an apprentice program for minority youths to learn the nearly lost art of stonemasonry, thus offering both a skill and a continuity with the best of the past; it also plans to turn the south transept into a giant bioshelter to show its commitment to the future and to new technologies. It has sponsored celebrations of other faiths (as well as a new age group), while remaining deeply true to its own Christian heritage. Thus, within the context of its dedication to the sacred, it spans past and future, traditional culture and new explorations.

There really is no single, universal model for a new age group. They come in all forms and sizes and engage in a multitude of activities. The book *Networking* lists over twelve hundred organizations, centers, cooperatives, groups, communities, and networks in fields ranging from health care and spiritual growth through politics, economics, and ecology, to education, communications, personal growth, and intercultural relations. There is hardly any area of human interest that does not have some people somewhere exploring it from a new age point of view.

As I said before, not all groups and organizations that call themselves "new age" truly embody the spirit of a new culture. Some use the term because it is glamorous to do so or it seems trendy. While it is true that, in one sense, we can say that everything ultimately contributes to the emergence of our future, to say that everything—or at least everything that espouses change or transformation—is new age is finally to say that nothing is. Some form of discernment between the genuine, the spurious, and the misleading is important if the concept of the new age or of new age groups is to have any significance.

I have already mentioned in a previous chapter some of my personal criteria for recognizing the spirit of emergence at work. I would add one more with respect to groups, and that is a willingness to be neutral, to create a context that empowers another group. It is the act of self-transcendence expressed at a group level, an openness to go beyond a particular group identity to allow a greater communion between persons and groups to take place.

Above all else, this has been what the Lorian Association has sought to explore: the consciousness of this larger cultural whole. When we created Lorian in 1973 after returning from Findhorn, we agreed that we would use our experience as a group to assist other groups, that we would not promote a particular Lorian work or teaching but that we would practice a neutrality that would allow other groups to meet us in a spirit of mutual empowerment. As it worked out, this approach did allow other new age groups to ac-

cept us into their midst as friends and helpers, feeling that
we would be no threat to them and would not try to steer
their course in our direction.

So complete was this trust that at one time two of our
members, Roger and Katherine Collis, accepted an invita-
tion to become administrators of another organization during a time of trouble it was passing through; they remained
with that organization for nearly two years before returning to Lorian. A number of us have spent weeks or months
living with other groups in the process of extending our
services.

Working in this way made it difficult for people to understand just who we were and what Lorian stood for,
which at times became a handicap. Our work often kept us
on the road, so we had no permanent center (although in
recent years we have gathered anew in Wisconsin, where
we have established an educational base). Our work has
borne fruit, however: we have been able to bring together
very different kinds of groups who otherwise might not
have found a point of contact with each other. We became, in effect, a networking organization, or more precisely, one dedicated to enhancing synthesis.

Synthesis is important to all the groups I have mentioned. It is, as I have said, one of the distinguishing characteristics of individuals and organizations that have taken
to heart the implications of the holistic paradigm, in which
all are one and also different. The new age is not a private
revelation nor a private possession, though there are organizations that behave as if that were so, claiming a certain
unique connection to the spiritual powers of the world.

I have mentioned the groups that I know best, the ones I
have been working with the most over the past few years.
They represent only a small fraction of all the formal and
informal groups, study meetings, organizations, schools,
and projects in some manner exploring the new age idea.
Most new age organizations work in areas of education,

counseling, personal growth, ecology, health care, and international issues. New age activities or projects are not as well represented in other areas, such as in the industrial sector, though there are signs that the new paradigm may be making inroads there, too.

One might not expect the military to be a scene of new age activity, but it is. Among the military men who are exploring a holistic world view and its implications for the military is Army Lieutenant Colonel Jim Channon, who has been developing the concept and training procedures for a new type of military unit which he calls the First Earth Battalion. Soldiers in this special group would be trained not only in the usual martial skills but also in other forms of conflict resolution and in spiritual disciplines. They would be "warrior monks," whose main mission would be to create harmony out of conflict by using techniques from meditation to force of arms, from ecological skills to humanistic psychology. The response to each situation would be unique, but the general strategy would be to seek to resolve conflicts through nonviolent spiritual and moral means first, with force of arms being the last option. For example, in confronting the American hostages' situation in Iran, the first response of the First Earth Battalion would have been an offer to exchange its soldiers for the hostages on a one-to-one basis.

Channon envisions the philosophy and training of this battalion as being open to anyone, civilian or military. In the First Earth Battalion training manual he says, "Those who strive after the truth and travel extensively in their quest are known as warriors. They are capable; they get the job done. Good soldiers are also known as warriors. The First Earth wants the action orientation of the warrior but tempered with the patience and sensitivity and ethics of the monk. These are the soldiers who have the power to make paradise. Why go for anything less?"

Channon has his supporters, but it is only fair to say that

he represents a visionary, minority position within the armed services. However, from just such seeds transformations can come.

The new world view has yet to make wide inroads into politics, but even there it has its adherents. Lorian has cosponsored seminars for elected officials on transformational vision, and I have always been impressed with the quality of the men and women who have attended. Most have been county and state officials, such as John Vasconcellos, chairman of the Ways and Means Committee of the California Assembly, who is a perfect example of an individual doing pioneering work in bringing holistic values into the political process. In *A Liberating Vision* he describes his odyssey through the human potential movement and his attempts to synthesize his experiences in self-exploration with his life as a politician. There are also new age political organizations, such as the New World Alliance, which provides educational services to persons working at every level of government. However, the new age idea is not, nor should it be, a political ideology. It is a vision of emergence and potential open to people of any political persuasion.

Though much of the new world view is either emerging from or being supported by scientific research, as yet there are few scientific and engineering groups openly espousing the emergence of a new age. The New Alchemy Institute is made up of scientists working with new kinds of "soft" technology, and Lindisfarne has scientists as part of the Fellows, including James Lovelock and Lynn Margulis, the developers of the Gaia hypothesis. Neither organization, however, is engaged in basic scientific research.

New age groups may be previews, though they are unfinished ones, of a new world. This is certainly true of the organizations I have mentioned: they are all growing, still exploring; there is nothing final about any of them.

They represent social and spiritual evolution in action, not its achievement.

The people who create or join such groups are for the most part ordinary people who have a vision that the world can be better and who sense that they can contribute to that process. There is a stereotype left over from the sixties of the drug-addled tripper or the dropout contemplating his own soul to the exclusion of all else. The seventies brought the horror of Jonestown and the image of the megalomaniacal cult leader. Such persons do not represent the values and purposes of the emerging world view, any more than the repressive groups that claim biblical authority for their ideas (and which make up the majority of the cults operating in the United States) represent the grace and spirit of Christianity, evangelical or otherwise. In all my travels and working with new age groups, I have met very few of them.

Instead, most of the people I know and work with are well integrated, active human beings. They are deeply spiritual, such as Jim Morton of the cathedral and Fritz and Vivienne Hull of Chinook. They are outstanding scholars such as Bill Thompson or social activists such as Belden Paulson—who almost singlehandedly created new communities in Sardinia and Italy to house and feed refugees after the Second World War, held a leadership position with the United Nations refugee program, and years later developed the first Peace Corps training program for President Kennedy.

The qualities these people have are not rare among the people who inhabit "Another America"; the world they co-create will be an exciting place to live in.

14

Building Community

Community is traditionally the birthplace of culture. Ancient and modern civilizations were seeded out of a rich welter of religious brotherhoods, pioneers' settlements and strategically placed communities that later flowered into villages and full-grown cities. It is within community that new values, ideals and lifestyles are being conceived and explored. It is community that gives meaning and coherence to culture. It is like the bamboo that helps the young sapling grow straight.

THUS WROTE MY FRIEND FRANÇOIS DUQUESNE IN *The New Times Network*, an international guidebook to new age groups. François is a Frenchman who arrived at the Findhorn community while I was still living there. At the time he was shy and bookish, knowledgeable about the esoteric traditions but not too skilled with people, perhaps because he could not speak English well. A decade later he is the official head of Findhorn (Peter Caddy having left to pursue other projects in North America), a world traveler and articulate speaker on many matters pertaining to culture and its emergence, and a respected leader within the new age milieu. When it comes to writing about community, François knows what he is talking about.

Whenever one reads about the vision of an emerging culture, the concept of community reappears over and over again. It is an affirmation of the spirit of connectedness; it is the living practice of communion. Many people, when thinking of becoming part of the new age milieu, think of joining or starting a community. Chinook calls its year-long program "core studies for building an Earth Community"—the community being both the one we all share by virtue of being human and the ecological community we share through our connectedness with Gaia. Earth Community becomes a synonym for the planetary culture at the heart of the new age image.

During the seventies, people observed the excesses of the human potential and growth movements and the focus many individuals put on their own fulfillment at the expense of others. The counterculture popularized the notion of "doing your own thing," and the images of "me-centeredness" and narcissism have inevitably become associated with the new age image. There is some validity in this view, to be sure, but it overlooks the equally strong movement toward community. Many communes and communities have indeed foundered on the rocks of self-centeredness, but others have survived because the principles of a

caring commitment to other people were seen as a necessary complement to practices of self-development.

Modern intentional communities have been created for
any number of reasons: for mutual economic support, for
religious purposes, for exploration of political ideologies,
and (among survivalists) for defense. Those creating new
age communities have still another reason. Community, as
François has pointed out, is the seedbed of culture, and the
seedbed is where seeds are nourished.

A community is not necessarily a group of people living
by and for themselves, somewhat separate from the rest of
society, following their own beliefs and doing their own
thing: community can take many forms. A community can
be a neighborhood within a city. It can be coworkers
within a corporation or industry. It can be a school or
members of an association. It can be a family. It can be two
people: the couple as community. The spirit of community
can even live in just one person, in whom the sense of a
loving and caring connectedness with all life is present.
Whether in the classrooms where he teaches, the office
where he works, or just out in society, my father creates
community wherever he goes through his openness and accessibility to people.

Indeed, community has to start with one person. People
simply living together are not necessarily a community (as
many families can testify); it takes mutuality—the willingness to be connected, to take on another's well-being, to
recognize oneself in the other. My invisible friend John has
often commented that the soul is a community, being the
love that experiences directly the wholeness of creation,
that nourishes that wholeness in return, and consequently
cannot be cut off from the rest of life. My own inner experiences have confirmed that this is so.

A community may be residential, but it need not be. At
Findhorn, those of us who initiated the Lorian Association
lived together in a single center. When we returned to

North America, we decided not to create an American version of Findhorn because our work of serving other groups demanded a mobility that would conflict with the responsibilities of maintaining a residential center. Instead, we focused on what we called the "community of consciousness," the inner spirit of community that can live in one person. We sought to explore the nature and meaning of community in a nonresidential manner, especially since the majority of people do not and probably will not live in traditional intentional communities like Findhorn.

Communities tend to be small because they depend on familiarity and the interchange of face-to-face encounters. Communities are woven from personal social contracts of accountability and commitment. When too many people are involved, those contracts either break down or become impersonal. Accountability becomes institutionalized and community becomes bureaucracy.

Given a holistic world view and a culture that nourishes an inner spirit of connectedness, there may be no limits to the size of a community. It could be a city, perhaps a nation, even the world itself, as the term *earth community* implies—each part unique and honored, yet inwardly contiguous and accessible, through love, to every other part. This is also the image of the mystical body of Christ and of the all-embracingness of the Buddha nature, in which all creation is one. If this seems too mystical, then we must remember that science itself is revealing a universe as holistic and interwoven as anything any mystic ever saw.

When I journey inward to contact John, I have often experienced the capacity of consciousnesses to become part of a larger whole. One may enter in John's world a communion in which there seems no limit to the number of participants nor to the intimacy one feels with them. It may be argued that this is a different reality, unconstrained by considerations of time and space. But this is not what makes communion possible. It is simply a spirit of love, unob-

structedness to others, and a security about one's own identity because one feels firmly rooted in the presence of divinity. Indeed, the experience of the sacred is what opens
us to community and makes it possible, for God is the original and, ultimately, the one community in which we all
share.

This consciousness of being one with others—group consciousness—is considered by many to be one of the qualities
of the Age of Aquarius. Many new age communities see
one of their functions as providing a center for exploring
and developing this group consciousness. What this means
is often unclear, though what is implied is frequently some
kind of telepathy. I have known groups that, through meditation practices and exercises in dream sharing and extrasensory perception, try to create a kind of group mind.
Group consciousness, however, is not primarily ESP; it is a
sensibility born of the simple act of accessibility, the willingness to be there for another and to trust one's inner self
into the hands of another.

One of the challenges of new age communities is to find
the balance between the individual's needs and those of the
group. When group consciousness is seen as the goal, individual consciousness may suffer. Synergy, however, makes
possible a concept of mutual empowerment between the
person and the larger whole. Synergy exists when the community and the self act on each other's behalf and when
neither seeks an undue advantage over the other.

Synergy is in some ways a political notion, but the creation of synergy is more than an issue of governance.
Groups may practice consensus politics and still not be
synergistic: a hidden politics of competition and struggle
between the individual and the group may still exist beneath the surface. It is not an easy issue and represents one
of the key areas of exploration in which new age communities are engaged.

Many groups, not just new age ones, are formed by

strong, dynamic personalities around whom issues of domination, submission, and competition naturally swirl, even
when unrecognized. Group consciousness may become simply a code word for agreement with the leader's perspectives. It is in this area as much as any other that a group's
efforts to embody the new paradigm may break down. It
may present all the right images and still embody an internal style of governance that is repressive and nonholistic.

Findhorn was particularly fortunate in this regard.
Though it is now governed by an interlocking series of internal groups and committees, with François as overall coordinator (officially he is chairperson of the core group),
the community was initially run by Peter Caddy, usually
acting on the spiritual guidance his wife, Eileen, received
in meditation. Peter is one of the most dynamic, forceful
leaders I have ever met, a vital man who resembles Pope
John Paul II in both his physical features and the vibrancy
of his personality.

If ever anyone could have dominated a community, it
was Peter. Yet he didn't. He equated authority with responsibility, and because he was always willing to take the responsibility (particularly the blame when things went
wrong), he had no hesitation about exercising authority.
What he did not do was hold it to himself, and if he found
others willing to share the accountability, then he shared
his authority, delegated his power, and empowered them to
be leaders, too. As Findhorn grew larger and more complex, he delegated more, until eventually he deliberately
eased himself out, having developed a strong community
to take on a collective responsibility and a collective authority.

Fritz and Vivienne Hull of the Chinook community are
servant leaders, as well. They are both much less forceful
as personalities than Peter Caddy but equally strong in
their ability to take responsibility and to embody a vision.
Indeed, their leadership is less one of taking charge than of

making the vision of Chinook and the new paradigm a living one in their own lives. They express a spirit clearly and provide the point of synthesis around which the community can coalesce. From the inspiration of their example, they empower and inspire others.

One of my favorite books is *Watership Down*, by Richard Adams. It is a fable of a group of rabbits on a dangerous quest to find a new home. Among this daring band are a number of specialists: one rabbit is an exceptionally strong warrior, one is a mystic and seer, one is very intelligent and clever. However, as individuals they are unable to work together well, because their very strengths tend to compete. Their leader, a rabbit named Hazel, has none of their strengths. He is neither the strongest, the fastest, the most clever, nor the most intuitive. He is simply the one who can synthesize the others; he can empower them to act as a wholeness.

To paraphrase Dr. Lynn Margulis's findings on cell evolution, the race does not always go to the swiftest nor evolution to the most strong; it is the symbiote, the one who is accessible to blending with others, who can synthesize the unique and the different and come up with a community of effort, who survives and prospers. There are many Hazels in the Aquarian conspiracy, for the capacity to be a Hazel is in large measure what that conspiracy is about, at least in political and social terms.

Dealing with this issue of synergy and the relationship between the individual and the group has been very important in Lorian. When we created the Lorian Association, we made it a principle that no one could be dependent on the group as a source of identity. No one could draw authority from being a member, only from his or her own inner spiritual source. At one point, when we felt the group experience was becoming a threat to individual development and strength, we dissolved the group for two years. We continued an association with each other as good

friends but undertook no collective projects, except our
continuing work of serving other groups when invited to
do so. At the end of the two years there was a mutual realization that we had all grown and developed in our sense
of inner authority and identity, and from the strength of
that development we resurrected Lorian.

In Lorian we have no single leader, but it would be
wrong to say we operate by consensus. What we seek to be
sensitive to is the "leadership function." Any Lorian can be
the point of synthesis and envisioning, the "leader." We
have an organizational structure that is conventional (a
president, vice-president, treasurer, secretary, and so forth)
but that is a structure of implementation, not one for making policy. Instead, we recognize each other's diverse skills
and authority in different areas, and we strive to be aware
when an individual is truly speaking from the spirit we all
share. In that moment he or she is the "leader." This person
may then, for that issue, be the authority, or the decision
may unfold through a group process. The question for us is
not group consciousness versus hierarchy but sensitivity to
the moving spirit of our community and the creation of
synergy. Leadership is seen as a function rather than a role.

One of the challenges that can obstruct a new age
group's capacity to create community is the glamour of the
new age idea itself and too great a sense of mission. Community becomes seen as a tool, a means to an end, which
might be transformation or the development of group consciousness or the discovery of new cultural forms. In the
midst of all this messianic work little room is left for the
human spirit or for conviviality. Such a community may be
an interesting place to visit, but you would not want to live
there.

In the urgency to achieve, the needs of the group may
well be seen as having priority over those of the individual.
There is a fine balance to be struck here. There are times
when the individual must sacrifice his or her own desires to

group needs; there are times when the reverse is true. Most of the time, the situation is probably not that critical. One important ingredient is humor. Findhorn has always been especially strong on this point, possessing a great talent for poking fun at itself and its problems. The community that can laugh at itself is more likely to achieve the balance it seeks. Pretentiousness about the new age is to be avoided at all costs.

One reason new age communities often run into trouble is that people do become obsessed with the vision. They have an image of emergence and want to be involved. Community seems an ideal vehicle for that involvement, but if community is seen as land, buildings, living together, or organization, the emphasis goes toward building a center rather than developing relationships.

After I returned from Findhorn in 1973, I was approached by a city planner who had an option on an excellent piece of land overlooking San Francisco Bay and wished to design a new age community. Knowing of my experience at Findhorn, he wanted my advice. He had extensive blueprints and plans; each home would be an electronic marvel, while everything was designed to honor the ecology of the land itself. What he lacked were people to buy and live in his houses, to be the community.

Nothing came of his plan, but his approach seems to be a common one. People are impatient; they want to start big, forgetting that community is not so much a place as a spirit. It is a miracle of relationship that needs to be nourished, a seed that needs time to develop. To build a new age community, one needs to start with the people and, in simple ways at first, explore the depths and limits of their accessibility to each other and their willingness to trust, to care, and to be there. Then the community will emerge, perhaps faster than one might anticipate.

Finally, there is another form of community: networking. Networking between groups and individuals may be one of the primary forms of the future for meeting both economic and political needs. Networking may be simply a matter of exchanging mailing lists, or it may be an evolution of a community of communities, a loosely organized association of groups. Lorian, Chinook, Lindisfarne, High Wind, Interface, and the cathedral of St. John the Divine are exploring such association. However it develops, the spirit behind networking and the potential it carries for large-scale communion and action may well represent the next important step in the emerging culture.

15

Novus Ordo Seclorum

ON ONE OF MY TRIPS TO WASHINGTON I WAS INVITED TO ATTEND
a small meeting with pollster Lou Harris, during which he
pointed out that the number one issue in the United States
as of the fall of 1982 was nuclear disarmament. Further, he
said, this issue cut across all of the normal divisions in our
country: over eighty percent of the American population—
Democrats, Republicans, and Independents; Conservatives
and Liberals; rich and poor; black, white, Chicano, and Ori-
ental; men and women—all agreed that all nuclear weapons
should be eliminated from the earth.

In the cause of preventing a nuclear war, people involved in new age work do the same kinds of things that
any other citizens may do. They march, they picket, they
write letters to their politicians, they vote on nuclear freeze

referendums, they become involved in whatever way their consciences dictate. The same is true for other issues: a number of the groups in the Aquarian network originated as antiwar, antinuclear, or ecological groups.

What, though, can the new world view offer that is different in the arena of world issues? Primarily, it is a change of perspective, which can offer a deeper analysis of our challenges, from which different strategies may come. It is important to remember, though, that the new age vision is not a set of answers as much as a change of direction in which to look for answers. It is still up to us to do the looking.

A friend of mine, William Becker, a journalist with a local newspaper, pointed out in *The Indefensible Society* (Lorian Press, 1981) that America's dependence on an overly centralized energy network made it vulnerable to either attack or terrorism. A shift to a more decentralized system that relied more on the local generation of energy through solar and wind power would make the United States much less vulnerable and much more defensible. (Another friend of mine in California recently built a fully solar powered house. Not only does she meet all her own energy needs but she sells a surplus back to the local power utility. Imagine neighborhoods of such houses, all acting as decentralized community generating stations. Not only would it be ecologically and economically more sound, it presents an unwinnable situation to any potential enemy. How could such a foe cripple America's energy capacity without attacking every house in the country?)

Such a shift is natural when seen through the eyes of the new paradigm, which encourages decentralization, empowering of the individual, a wider distribution of power, and the use of renewable resources as a way of living "lightly" upon the earth. By reducing a national sense of vulnerability, it reduces the level of tension and fear, from which conflict can arise. A decentralized society is far easier to de-

fend than one that is structured around a few key centers
of industry, energy, and communications, and a society that
is easier to defend is much less likely to be attacked.

A holistic world view also encourages what anthropologist Gregory Bateson called "systemic wisdom," the wisdom
of knowing how the different parts of life interweave and
interact as a wholeness. To a great degree, many of the
problems we face in our world are the result of acting toward parts of life as if they were unconnected to other
parts. We are learning through the negative feedback of
environmental pollution just how wrong this type of re-
ductionist thinking and acting is.

When systemic wisdom is applied to the great issues of
our time, it quickly becomes apparent that they cannot be
dealt with as separate problems. Yet that is precisely how
we try to deal with them. We treat the problems of nuclear
weapons, global poverty, and environmental pollution as
if they were separate projects, which can be assigned
different priorities. Yet, these problems have common roots
that affect each other. John has described this situation:

> The alienation from nature, the conflict between cultures
> and societies, the threat of nuclear war, the stress of
> world economies: all these reflect the development of
> selfhood unintegrated with the spirit of synthesis. They
> also all represent the pressure of that spirit toward that
> integration. Because these challenges are greater than a
> single individual or a single country can solve, they in-
> voke a global awareness and the possibility of a global
> response from you.

Without minimizing the absolute necessity of ridding our
world of nuclear weapons, it is still true that this is a glamour issue. A nuclear bomb is immediately threatening to
the average citizen of an industrialized country. Hunger
and world poverty are less so. Children starving in Africa,

hovel cities in Latin America, or refugee camps in the Middle East are less frightening to well-fed people across the ocean than Russian ICBM's. Nearly a million people can march on behalf of a nuclear freeze, but would that many march on behalf of feeding the people of the world? More importantly, would they make a continuing personal sacrifice to see that resources of money and food were available for such a purpose and to take the important first steps toward redressing the balance of abundance upon the earth?

We fear a nuclear holocaust, but millions of individuals in the poor nations of the world are living in a holocaust of disease, poverty, starvation, and death right now. In a holistic world, their suffering is ours as well; it is a despair, a scream, in the soul of humanity that affects all of us. If a war comes, it will be born out of that despair, not out of politics or economics, though those might seem the surface reasons. It would come because at a deep level humanity had given up hope and had been overwhelmed by its own pain.

Our new world view is fundamentally transnational. It can recognize threats to the well-being of all of Gaia, but it does not cast certain nations into the role of villain. It sees that the enemies of the earth are in every nation, as are its friends. Both communist and capitalist systems are still fundamentally oriented to the industrial paradigm, which, for all its undoubted successes, is now reaching certain limits and producing excesses that threaten all of us. The challenge facing humanity is beyond economic ideologies.

While alerting us to the big picture, the holistic perspective alerts us to the small one as well. It tells us that the power of each person to affect the whole cannot be measured by that person's quantitative influence—the number of people he knows, his social position, his wealth—but by the quality of his thought and actions. When we think of the transformation of history and culture, we think quite naturally (for that is how our cultural tradition trains us to think) of large-scale actions, such as those that presidents and prime ministers, popes and pop stars can take. Since most of us do not occupy such lofty positions, we are, in consequence, disempowered.

In the holistic world view, as in the spiritual world view, each individual life resonates its qualities into the whole in a manner that affects every other part of life. It is the analogy of Rupert Sheldrake's morphogenetic fields and his principle of morphic resonance. Each person's act of charity, of love, of empowerment, of connectedness, enhances the capacity of all of us to take such actions. I may not be able to address Congress or the Politburo, but I can act to make my own life and my connections—my work, my family, my environment—qualitatively whole in themselves and life-giving to others. Further, there is no way of knowing how a simple act, taken in faith, can have unforeseen repercussions, perhaps even an effect on the Congress or the Politburo. History is filled with examples of such a principle at work. There is no reason to suppose it has stopped working now.

It is a mistake to look to the emerging culture and say, "Because you dare to claim a new vision, you must have answers for our old problems." Often, it cannot provide blueprints because it is in the process of discovering itself. If we wish solutions, we must be prepared to put the new world view to work in our lives and hearts and help in that process of cultural discovery ourselves. Out of that may well come the answers we are seeking.

Hundreds of thousands of people have already been touched in some way by this new perspective and given an enlarging and empowering sense of themselves. They are learning to be more open, more sensitive, more caring; they are learning to see issues in a new way and to discover in equally new ways their own capacities to act on behalf of humanity. This is a growing power for good in our world, which unfortunately receives little recognition in the media. It will definitely make its mark over the next two decades and beyond.

Furthermore, this growing force is worldwide. It is true that in some ways the new age idea has peculiarly North American overtones. There are reasons for this: the United States is still the preeminent industrial and technological nation in the world; it is not surprising that the focus of a paradigm shift would be in this country. Also, America was founded on a vision of transformation. On the back of the Great Seal of the United States, reprinted on every dollar bill, are the words *novus ordo seclorum,* "a new order of the ages." To be "new age," to be a country created on behalf of the future of all humanity, is very American. Canada shares this vision, and is also a profoundly planetary country, engaging in its own experiment of exploring and creating a multicultural society.

Images of transformation and the efforts to implement them are spread throughout the globe. New age groups and communities are on every continent, seeing themselves as part of a transnational network, exchanging insights, ideas, personnel. My Lorian colleague Milenko Matanovic was the founder of a spiritual and artistic community in his homeland of Yugoslavia. The Soviet interest in parapsychology is well known; less well known is that Soviet scientists are also engaged in defining a new paradigm of the universe and coming to the same conclusions about its holistic nature as their western counterparts.

Michael Murphy, founder of the Esalen Institute, has been making trips to Russia to contact its burgeoning human potential movement and the scientists exploring the new visions of reality. In an interview with Keith Thompson in the March 1982 issue of *New Age,* he says:

[There are] profound changes happening in the Soviet Union that have generally gone unreported by the Amer-

ican media and unnoticed by professional Soviet watch-
ers. [It is] a cultural awakening . . . not unlike the
awakening in America in the 1960s, though it's far more
quiet. A growing subculture there is exploring esoteric
religions, gestalt and encounter groups, alternative healing methods, UFOs, the search for lost continents, parapsychology. As in the '60s in the United States, the exploration ranges from the sublime to the ridiculous, but
what unites it all is a growing conviction among many
Soviet citizens and scientists that hidden human reserves
must be discovered and developed.

All over the world people are exploring the level of reality on which humanity may meet in oneness, the level
where Gaia awaits the maturing of her "nervous system."
The roots of this movement are in the perennial philosophy, the common holistic and esoteric wisdom at the heart
of every culture throughout history. Its influence has yet to
be fully felt. When it is, however, it will not be just an
influence on single issues, no matter how vital those issues
may be, but on the connections between these issues. It
will be an influence on the central challenge we face, one
that is deeper than nuclear armament, deeper than pollution, deeper than world hunger because ultimately it is the
source of these problems. That is the need for human consciousness to evolve, to develop the wisdom and spirit necessary to harness the awesome powers of atom and gene,
psyche and intuition, that we are liberating.

16

The Mystical Emergence

The central spiritual fact in our world is that we enter a time of a deeper incarnation of divinity within the earth. We experience this as the approach of a great life, a presence of immense light and love. This new approach will not be through a single individual but through all humanity.

THESE WORDS OF MY FRIEND JOHN, PUBLISHED BY LORIAN IN *Cooperation with Spirit,* lead us into the final aspect of the new age which we need to consider: the unfoldment of the mystical dimension of planetary life.

Because my childhood contact with that dimension was
my entry point into the whole idea of an emerging new culture, this is the aspect that stands out for me: the liberation
of a greater spiritual presence within society and the renaming of the sacred. When this is achieved, every act,
every connection in our lives can become sacramental.

The new age idea has spiritual overtones: many of its
roots lie in prophetic revelation. Some people come to this
idea with a religious fervor worthy of any crusade; such
people make spiritual development an integral part—if not
the whole—of the new age experience.

But the emerging paradigm is not a new religion. It is
more a mystical or holistic sensibility that is in alignment
with the essential teachings and mystical traditions of all
the great world religions. Though they are often equated,
mysticism and religion are not the same thing. Mysticism is
the experience of the wholeness in which we are embedded
—the perception of the presence of God. It is an experience
of unity with that presence, the discovery of the spirit of
God within oneself. Religion deals with external acts of
worship and behavior, the process of honoring, supplicat-
ing, or pleasing an external deity. Religions often show us
how we are different from God and dependent upon the
divine presence for our very existence; mysticism shows us
how we are one with God and coparticipants with divinity
in the unfoldment of creation. Both these perceptions are
important. They are complementary. They have also been
perceived as conflicting, and there is a long history in every
religion of the struggle between the mystical and the dog-
matic points of view.

In its humanistic, scientific, and spiritual aspects, the
new paradigm leans toward a mystical perspective, though
not necessarily at the expense of the religious one. The
awareness it offers of the intercommunal nature of life can
enrich and empower the religious experience while at the
same time liberating from purely institutional or theolog-

ical contexts the complementary experience of the spirituality of life itself. An everyday encounter with the sacred in no way precludes the formal worship of divinity.

The quest for a greater experience of the sacred or for a more spiritual culture is hampered by a certain spiritual illiteracy, a lack of understanding of what spirituality is, that distorts and obscures this mystical side of the new age perspective. This illiteracy takes many forms, such as believing that spirituality is something that only clergy need deal with or that it is "otherworldly" and unrelated to practical affairs.

One form this lack of understanding can take in the new age milieu is the confusion between psychic phenomena and spirituality itself. Psychic powers, or ESP (extrasensory perception), the existence of which are gradually receiving the acceptance of science, are modes of perception beyond the five senses. They perhaps represent ways of tapping into Bohm's "implicate order" or Pribram's "holonomic domain," in which all knowledge is everywhere available unrestricted by space or time.

Psychic abilities, such as telepathy and remote distance viewing, which transcend the boundaries of space and time as we know them, can offer us a threshold experience of the wholeness that pervades the universe. However, they are not usually thought of in such mystical terms. Psychic talents have a glamour that makes them good subjects for drama and a desirous commodity. Much of the glamour, however, derives from the motivation to be special and different, to have power over life. The very fact that these capacities are usually called psychic "powers" and not psychic "perceptions" or "senses" says something about how we perceive and value them.

It is one thing to have psychic experiences, such as telepathically sharing thoughts with another mind or clairvoyantly seeing an event in a time or place remote from us, and something else entirely to practice connectedness. If

we do not think and act holistically and caringly with the
information we receive from our five physical senses, there
is no guarantee that we shall suddenly begin to do so with
more information from more and different senses.

The development of psychic abilities—the abilities that
will enable humanity to share some kind of communal
mind with nature, or Gaia—may be a part of a future culture. Such abilities could be used destructively, however, if
not combined with a well-developed moral sense. Certain
mind-development groups teach that these abilities cannot
be used except in moral ways, but my experience has been
that this is not true. Invasion of privacy, the domination of
one mind by another, and a completely false assumption of
authority or superiority based on having psychic contact
with invisible worlds are among the misuses of psychic
gifts that I have seen, not to mention the distortion, the
delusions, and the mental and emotional imbalance that
can come when a personality is unable to integrate psychic
experiences in a healthy and grounded way or becomes
obsessed by their glamour.

I believe continuing research into parapsychology and
the untapped resources of the human mind is important.
This is not the same as developing spirituality, however. It
is no substitute for putting holistic insights to work in our
lives. We do not need more perceptions and powers to
begin the *practice* of connectedness in loving, wise, and
caring ways. At the heart of spirituality is a relationship
with God, a covenant that holds both parties accountable
in a bond of love, and then extends this love and accountability in nourishing and empowering ways into our relationships with each other and our world. Simple perception
or the receiving of information, however exotic the method,
is not such a covenant. It holds us to no bond of accountability to and for each other, though it can serve such a
bond. The person who claims spiritual authority because of
a psychic talent or the person who sees the presence of

spirit in every act of ESP forgets this, and forgetting, continues in a delusion that is far from the holistic reality he seeks.

Psychic abilities are often seen as forms of power, but spirit itself is also often identified with power. People look to spirit for guidance, for help, for intervention, seeing it as a source of power external to themselves. Spirit and its power are then not seen as existing in and emerging from the relationships and connections of life but as a separate special state, much as we might see the presidency or a monarchy. Spirituality, when seen in such a context, takes on similar trappings of extraordinariness. We fail to see it in the ordinary transactions and events of our days but expect it to manifest itself in robes and clouds and halos of splendor and magnificent power.

When this occurs, the sensibility toward the mystical domain is obscured by images of spiritual intervention and displays of power. From my own perceptions and from my experience with John, I believe there is an active participation by the spiritual worlds in human affairs. Such involvement is protective, healing, and nourishing of our unfoldment and represents the circulation of life and energy between all the parts of the holistic world order, both physical and nonphysical. Such participation is generally anonymous and low-key, working invisibly through inspiration and the activity of men and women of good will throughout the world. Any of us can be open to such a partnership with spiritual forces, for they are invoked to us by our own capacities to perceive the needs of humanity and to act in appropriate and skilled ways.

Throughout western history, however, there has often appeared a different view of spiritual intervention, one which some aspects of the new age movement, drawing on the historical character of millennarian movements in general, have also picked up. This is the expectation that spirit can and should "do it for us" in some magical way. This might be expressed as "if God [or whatever a person's image of a supremely powerful spiritual source might be] is so powerful and good, then He should do something about the world and change it to a better state."

This attitude assumes that, in fact, nothing is being done, when the truth is that we may simply be unable to recognize the help we are receiving. For all the painful and fearful things in our world, it might be much worse if we were not—and had not been over the years—receiving a full measure of assistance and protection from the spiritual worlds.

It also assumes that spirit is all-powerful and that we have no responsibility or power ourselves in the matter. It does not recognize the manner in which, in a holistic universe, we are also part of that spirit. If the goal were only an act of transformation, the need to change one thing into another, then an intervention might work. However, if our destiny is social and spiritual maturation and the realization of our own creative participation in the way in which the world manifests itself, then no one can do it for us. No one can mature us; we must do that ourselves by confronting the problems of our own making and correcting them. Spirit's role—the role of spirituality—is to empower us to accomplish this and thereby discover the inner power we each have to fulfill the responsibilities we all share for the well-being of our world.

The interventionist outlook takes different forms. It can appear in an overreliance on guidance from spiritual sources (and in a plethora of people willing to provide it—as John has said, there are persons on both sides of the line between the visible and invisible worlds who are only too happy and willing to tell others what to do). This comes from the idea that spirit, being spirit, knows better than we what we should be doing; the emphasis is on obedience, not on cocreativity.

It can also appear in the guise of various individuals who claim to be messiahs and avatars (divine teachers, according to Hindu philosophy). While highly inspired people who are true spiritual adepts are undoubtedly working in our world, the characteristics of most of those who publicly lay claim to that identity are a fascination with power and a flamboyant life-style. They seem less intent on being servant leaders and more on gathering followers who will give them obedience, equating numbers of bodies in attendance upon their teachings with their power to change the world.

These "avatars" need not be individuals, nor do they always come cloaked in spiritual trappings. They can be groups, associations, corporations; they can present themselves simply as the new experts, the new managers who will give us detailed blueprints on how to straighten out the world. Their power lies in our cultural reliance on experts, who can be useful and important but who can suffer from tunnel vision, restricted by the boundaries of their own specialties and at times by their own desire for influence. As Norman Cousins, former editor of *Saturday Review*, succinctly puts it in *Human Options*, "The biggest task of humanity in the next fifty years will be to prove the experts wrong."

The interventionist idea can appear closer to home as well, in the form of our children. The future of the new world view and of the emerging culture rests on those who will be its citizens. Adults already imbued with older perspectives face the challenge of change; children, however, can grow naturally into the holistic outlook. Not knowing any other, for them the new age can be simply the age that is. For this to happen, however, means pioneering appropriate forms of education both in school and in the home, such as the transcultural education I discussed in Chapter 5, and nourishing the unfoldment of a proper sense of the sacredness and wholeness of life.

It is easier for children to grasp this holistic awareness since their world is initially perceived as being more interconnected. They are not born knowing the artificial boundaries and limits that adults impose upon reality. They have a native mystical sensibility. Because of this, those who believe in the intervention of spirit sometimes see in our children the very avatars that will save us, souls fresh from God and filled with insight. This can even go to the extreme of parents (and I have known some of them) claiming their son or daughter to actually be the Avatar come to save humanity. Such children are then burdened with expectations, pressured to show insights and wisdom far beyond their years.

Children can have insights that adults lack or have lost. For all their freshness of vision, however, they do not have the wisdom that comes from experiencing the world, nor the integration of the self that comes with maturity. To put them in the role of special entity is to deny them the chance to be ordinary, to make mistakes, to become truly incarnate in the world as it is; it is to short-circuit the maturing process.

In my own case, whenever I did share my particular insights with my parents, they always honored them but treated them as something natural and ordinary. They gave me the gift of a childhood that did not have to live up to any special image in spite of any unusual psychic or mystical gifts I may have shown from time to time. It was not until I was a teenager that others whom we met began to deal with me as if I were something special because of my inner attunement.

By that time, fortunately, I already had a sense of personal integration and perspective that allowed me to deal with those projections without glamour. This integration, however, was due in large measure to the wisdom of my parents in demonstrating daily the naturalness of the sacred. They taught me the secret of what I call the "divinely ordinary" and made sure that whatever mystical leanings I had did not separate me from the world or from others. This they did simply by making such leanings a natural part of everyday human life and showing that spirituality, like breathing, was a normal and necessary part of being alive. They taught that spirituality was not confined to a church or a particular religion but was discovered in daily actions of love and compassion, in communication with others and with the world, in a reverencing for life.

In every generation, children do represent an intervention by spirit in our history; they are the potential of the newborn in our midst. They have qualities of insight which, arising from fresh minds, can expand our own awarenesses of our world and remind us of our own capacities for freshness. On the other hand, to expect them to be miracle workers or to elevate them to a special position is to deny the very gifts they can offer. It is to make them screens for our own projections of need and desire and to mold them in our own fantasies of power.

In whatever form it takes, the interventionist philosophy, with its images of spirit as power, denies the promise of spirit as connectedness. It obscures the mystical dimension of our life and our participation in that dimension and is ultimately disempowering. It says that the challenge before us of creating a better future is too big for humanity, that we are good at making messes but unable to clean up after ourselves. In my experience, this is a misleading and hopeless point of view, making us vulnerable to individuals and groups that would take power from us to serve their own visions, which are rarely the vision of the whole. Instead, I see us as mature enough to accept responsibility and capable enough to work with ourselves, our world, and our spiritual connections to make a difference. If spirit is to intervene, then it will be in partnership with us, acting through our attunement and our efforts, our compassion and our wisdom.

There is a final way in which the new age represents the emergence of the mystical dimension. This is in the birth of a new consciousness. John has stated from time to time that the new age is an act of planetary incarnation, the birth of a planetary mind and soul. In this view, humanity is at the threshold not just of cultural change but of an evolutionary leap. Through the growing complexity and intimacy of our global connections, a new level of awareness altogether, a new mind, a new consciousness will emerge. What this new state will be like cannot now be predicted, though I feel it will be similar to that condition of intuitive blending and insight that we now call mystical. I know it will not be a group mind in the sense that individuality will be suppressed; indeed, the experience of our individual identities and creativity will be enhanced. However, it will be a state of mind that encompasses more than just humanity and will reach out and connect with the wider "mind" of nature as a whole. It will be a true Gaia mind, for which humanity, as Lovelock speculates, will be the nervous system and the focus of self-awareness. The experience of this state will redefine what we mean by nature, humanity, and spirit, synthesizing all three into a mystical body of planetary life and unfoldment.

In this way, the new age is the emergence of a new revelation, a new covenant between God and the wholeness of planetary life. It is the mystical birth of a new being, a new expression of divinity, whose life is our life—all our lives. The paradigm shift is our coming to realize that we are both the cradle and the body for that birth.

17

Shadows of Aquarius

CARL JUNG IDENTIFIED THE PRINCIPLE OF *enantiodromia*, THE tendency of human actions and intentions to turn into their opposite. Thus, an act of healing may result in a patient's becoming more ill; a social reform, such as prohibition, may result in the emergence of new crimes and criminals. William Irwin Thompson draws upon this concept in *Evil and World Order:* "It is no longer safe to assume that good intentions are enough. One can wreak havoc with benevolence as well as with malevolence."

In concluding our swift passage along the brink, it may be useful to see what *enantiodromia* might await us in our pursuit of a new age. Proponents of the Age of Aquarius picture it as an emerging era of light and enlightenment, but what are some of its shadows along the way?

I have already mentioned in passing some of the distortions and imbalances one is likely to find: a desire for power, the tyranny of the group over the individual in the name of community, glamour, an attachment to novelty for its own sake, a withdrawal from the world. Many of the shadows of Aquarius are the same human failings one finds in any enterprise. Where people become narrowly committed to an idea and lose the perspective of larger interconnectedness, there is the tendency for foolishness, for callousness, for self-righteousness, and for extremism. The new age movement has no special protection against these tendencies except the ordinary vigilance of people not to be caught by them. Anyone journeying to "the edge of history" should do so with a keen sense of discernment and discrimination.

Some of the special distortions in this area arise from the millennarian nature of new age expectations—distortions of how we act in history. They arise from images of liberation, breakthrough, and transcendence, particularly as applied to issues of creativity and power. They have in common the desire not to be limited by anything, not by the past, by the future, by circumstances, or by others.

For many, the new age means the breaking of boundaries, the achievement of a new liberation of spirit and emotions. This is particularly true for those in the human potential movement. In its best form, humanistic psychology seeks to break through unwarranted and pathological limits upon our inner potential. At its worst—or at its least understood and integrated—it becomes a quest for limitlessness itself, regarded as essential for creativity and growth. The ordinary relationships of society, such as jobs, marriage, family, even the social covenant itself in the form of compassion, caring, and plain common courtesy, come to be seen as constrictions to be cast aside in the freedom to "do one's own thing." In the late sixties almost a quarter of the marriages I knew split up on grounds of "self-development."

The lure of limitlessness is found in other areas of human life and endeavor as well. For example, the whole conservationist and ecological movement is directed against the assumption of limitlessness in the industrial sphere. When it is taken for granted that human beings are above and beyond natural limits, then we lose the capacity to relate realistically to our finite world. Unfortunately, even as the new age movement speaks of honoring the limits of the earth, some elements within it continue to foster and pursue the idea of limitlessness itself. This can continue to distort our relationship to the earth and to other kingdoms of life. It can also distort our understanding of spirituality, leading to the erroneous view of spirituality as a state of limitlessness achieved by throwing off the so-called constrictions and boundaries of our humanness.

This search for limitlessness is an example of what Alfred North Whitehead calls "misplaced concreteness." It is the attempt to express an infinite quality within a finite world. It is true that there are qualities, such as love and compassion, which renew themselves by the act of giving—the more we use them, the more we have. Yet we give them in specific ways. It does no good to have a limitless love for humanity and not for individual human beings. The opposite of limitlessness is not confinement but focus and commitment. Without focus, without boundaries, we have chaos; we have cancer, not growth—an explosion, not a creative unfoldment. Thomas Berry identifies the quality of diversification—the creation of unique individualities—as one of the governing principles of the universe. This process, however, is not possible without limits, something that distinguishes me from you and the two of us from the beech tree outside my window.

One of the great mystical ideas, one that runs through many traditions, including Christianity (as, for example, in the writings of Meister Eckhart) is the idea of an inner divinity, that God which lives within each of us and bestows upon us each a portion of the gift of creativity. It is a sacred idea, affirming us as participants and partners in the ongoing unfoldment of creation. This idea is also a central one in the emerging scientific view that we live in a participatory universe.

This idea has been taken over by pop psychology and humanistic training groups and expressed as the philosophy that we create our own worlds. There is truth in this idea, and at its best it leads us to take responsibility for our experiences. It can also empower us with a sense of our capacity to transform our lives. It puts us in touch with our ability to change and to grow.

However, this idea that we each create our own world can disconnect us from the rest of the world, allowing us to deny any responsibility for another's state of being. I have sat in groups where individuals have said they are not responsible for the suffering in the world since those who suffer have obviously chosen and created that experience. In the name of a "new" perception of divinity, all sense of the interconnectedness and wholeness of the world is lost.

The idea of the God within, improperly understood, can also make us lose sight of the other image of God as an external presence and force in the world. Instead of seeing ourselves as cocreators we imagine ourselves as creators. But what, then, can we create except forms in our own image? Where is the possibility of transformation in that? If the God within is not complemented by a living experience of God as that which transcends us, it becomes an idol, wrought in the image of our own personalities. We are then more limited than before, since we have lost a sense of that which can help us transcend ourselves.

We must remember that we are also *creatures*. We are not autonomous sources of change for our world. We are also among the ranks of that which is created and thus owes its existence to another source. We are created by our ecology, by nature, by the community in which we live, by the culture in which we have developed. We are created by the connections of love and friendship we form. We are created by God.

It is characteristic of a creature to have limits. Yet in these very limits, in this very dependency upon another source, lies true power and freedom. If we are the source, if we are the sole creative power in our lives, then when things go wrong, when we reach our limits, we have no place to turn. If, however, we recognize our creaturehood, then we recognize a source that can empower us to transcend our limits and change.

The desire to be free from limits takes other forms. It can, for example, result in a failure to be discriminating, an unwillingness to say that anything is out of place or wrong. There are often natural boundaries between people and groups, boundaries, for example, of interest, of technique and style of working, and of objective. There is a spirit of appropriateness which is ignored in the interest of casting out limits. I have seen new age groups sponsor conferences in which totally incompatible organizations are brought together in the name of synthesis and wholeness. The result at best is confusion and at worst actual conflict.

Without an ability to discriminate, no real creativity is possible. A friend of mine who is a concert cellist lived for many years in a spiritual community, and even organized a chamber music group of some excellence. She eventually had to leave because, in a fuzzy notion of empowerment, the community gave equal appreciation to any kind of musical effort on the part of anybody. It was all applauded and praised and considered perfect, from my friend's masterful renditions to the woman who would stand up and sing a song off key while forgetting most of the words. Without some form of appropriate critical feedback, my friend could not judge how she was doing as a musician.

To save her own creativity from a surfeit of uncritical praise, she had to leave.

True empowerment is not indiscriminate. We empower by pointing out mistakes as well as by praise and by affirming jobs well done. Recognition of quality is vital if a new culture is to emerge with any kind of standards of excellence, and that means imposing limits.

When everything is seen as perfect, nothing is. In an atmosphere where all is considered right just because it exists and a critical discernment is considered an imposition of limits, evil can flourish. Evil is, when all is said and done, a true imposition of limits. The limits that evil sets are always the wrong ones, the ones that disempower, that curtail, that collapse one into a tiny ball of true powerlessness. The limits that evil sets do not define us and give us a direction for growth; they are not limits out of which creativity can emerge.

For the new age to prosper, it needs people willing to accept the reality of their creaturehood, the value of certain kinds of limits, the blessing of definition; it requires people who with loving and vigorous minds and hearts can exercise a rigorous and loving discrimination, who can call a fault a fault and a mistake a mistake, not just a "learning experience." It needs people who can shake off the mind-numbing effects of psychobabble and jargon (unfortunately all too prevalent amidst the "Aquarian Conspiracy") and see and speak clearly, who can look evil in the eye and call it by its name. It needs people who know freedom because they understand their limits (and the limitlessness that comes only from communion and from God) and yet are not afraid to feel responsible for their world.

Perhaps the greatest shadow comes from the idea of the new age itself, or at least from the term. It can be a useful description, and one I have used deliberately in this book in order to give it a more precise definition. However, I don't use it much anymore in lecturing. The danger is the tendency to create an attitude of division, "old age" versus "new age." Worse, there can be an unwillingness to deal with history at all.

This can take different forms. On the one hand, it can result in an ignorance of the past, giving us too narrow a perspective. So much of new age thought and its images draw on millennarian expectations and traditions, such as the idea of apocalypse. Failure to see it as a recurrence of an old idea makes us more vulnerable to modern versions of that idea. Also, the new age movement in North America has much in common with its counterpart in Europe between the world wars. The ecological spirit and desire for transcendence expressed at that time in Germany became corrupted and channeled into the Nazi movement, which had many roots in occultism. We are in a different historical period, but an understanding of how this corruption occurred then can prevent it from happening now in new forms.

The other manifestation of an unwillingness to deal with history is a desire for results now. Many new age groups started in the sixties and early seventies with what I call a precipice mentality. Expectations were high that something was about to occur and the new age was imminent. Ordinary history was irrelevant since it was about to end anyway with the dawning of a new era. When this did not occur, there was a backlash. I remember one psychic, who had a national following, yelling with rage in her living room one day when a cycle of catastrophes she had been predicting for several years did not take place and she realized that our civilization was going to be around awhile longer. That was in the late sixties. More recently, I was talking with a man who wondered what had happened to the new age and whether it was worthwhile continuing with certain group projects that he had started. He did not have a sense of how much is involved in cultural change and was not really prepared for a lifetime's task.

By compressing all of meaningful history into the last quarter of the twentieth century, some in the new age movement lose the perspective of the long haul. The time for the precipice mentality has passed. In the eighties and nineties and beyond, if the new age idea is to have relevance, it must be translated into long-term projects of service to humanity; it must honor the emergence of a new culture, with the need to develop its own economic, political, educational, scientific, religious, and artistic perspectives and expressions. This development takes time, like any process of maturation. The new age is a process, not a sudden event.

I have sought to point out that emergence represents continuity and maturation as much as transformation. If we only seek what is new and different, we cut ourselves off from much of the heritage of humanity. We also cut ourselves off from the very momentum toward maturation that exists in our world. We may not like the world we are living in, but it is the product of someone's new age aspirations of centuries back. Compared to our ancestors (however much we may wish to romanticize the past) we in the industrialized world live in a paradise, and the potential exists to extend our abundance to all humanity.

That we also live in a time of great peril, when the contradictions within our industrial society collide with the contradictions in our own natures, is an example of the principle of *enantiodromia*. It does not mean that those who have gone before us have had any less of a desire, nor worked any less hard, to build a new world. It does mean we must learn from our history to become more conscious of our images, our actions, and their consequences. Otherwise, a hundred years from now, if we still survive as a species, another David Spangler will be writing another book about another movement to create a new age and finally give birth to the holistic civilization.

18

A Wild Dream

The starting point for a better world is the belief that it is possible. Civilization begins in the imagination. The wild dream is the first step to reality. Visions and ideas are potent only when they are shared. Until then, they are merely a form of daydreaming.

THIS IS ONE OF MY FAVORITE QUOTES FROM A FAVORITE BOOK, *Human Options* by Norman Cousins. It sums up the whole spirit of emergence very nicely. The new age is a "wild dream" beginning in the imagination. That dream is being

shared. It may not come to pass exactly as envisioned, but
it is no daydream.

What does a person do who wants to be part of this
dream and give it potency? How does one begin? How to
participate in emergence?

The doorways are all around us. There are books to read,
groups to contact, projects to get involved with.

The first doorway, though, is in ourselves, in our own
imaginations. What do we feel about the possibilities of a
new age? Can we imagine a holistic world, a caring world,
a world that is a great community of life? If so, then can
we imagine how we would act in such a world? If, through
some miracle, that new world came into being just this
second as you are reading these words, what would you be
like? What would you do, what actions would you take toward yourself and those around you that would be appropriate to that world?

In Russell Schweickart's words, we are asked to be "sensing elements." That is the first step: to see ourselves and to
see our world in a new context, just as an astronaut would
from orbit. All else flows from that vision of the whole
earth. All else flows from our imaginative perception of the
possibilities inherent in ourselves and in our world to experience a rebirth.

We can also reinterpret our history. The new age is not
just or even primarily transformation; it is evolution and
maturation. We are finally achieving a reverence for the
wholeness of Gaia, through which we may also be empowered. We are not the first generation to glimpse this or even
the first to act upon it to some degree; we will not be the
last. However, knowing we are part of a historical flow
does not detract from the uniqueness of this moment in
which we must imagine, dream, share—and act.

When my grandfather and my father stood on the hills
overlooking their farm and launched rockets into the sky,
they were dreaming their wild dreams. When a human be-

ing walked on the moon, those dreams found a fulfillment.

I have a dream, too, that one day we shall all walk this earth as if it were a new world—and in that time it will be new, for we will see it and ourselves with new eyes and touch each other with a new and gentle spirit. We will know the delight of the sacred within us and around us and the joy of being partners, cocreators, with the earth and with God. Whether my grandchild will witness the fulfillment of this dream is up to all of us.

Resource List

GETTING STARTED

Each person begins the exploration of emergence in his or her own unique way. For some it is through science, for some through religion and spiritual studies; for some it is through holistic health, for others through economic or political interests. Some people discover the idea of a coming age through books, while others are introduced through friends or by coming in contact with a particular group or center.

I have deliberately kept the following resource list very small, limiting it to groups with whom I am personally very familiar and to a select few books that I have used as texts in classes or have otherwise found helpful in my work. To

achieve a full list of the resources available would require
a book as large as this one is already. My own personal library on transformation, spirituality, and an emerging new
culture contains over seven hundred books, and it is far
from being complete. Fortunately most books have bib-
liographies that can lead an interested person onward in
his or her search. Likewise there are many more excellent
groups and organizations than just those listed below. The
groups I have mentioned, however, are all noteworthy in
helping people explore a full spectrum of ideas and possibilities connected with the new paradigm; they have no
dogmas themselves but seek to help individuals find their
own understanding and connection with the idea of an
emerging age. This makes them ideal starting points.

GROUPS

Bear & Company, Inc.
P.O. Drawer 2860
Santa Fe, New Mexico 87501
   This is a publishing house rather than a group. I include
it because it is the major source for books, tapes, and publications dealing with creation-centered spiritualities (including Celtic Christianity), one of the major spiritual
paths underlying the paradigm of emergence.

Chinook Learning Community
P.O. Box 57
Clinton, WA 98236
   Chinook is an educational community in the Pacific
Northwest. Its primary activities at the time of this writing
are sponsoring both long- and short-term educational programs about personal and social transformation, spirituality, and the emerging age, and creating an "eco-village," a
small community demonstrating a way of living in harmony
with the values of ecology and the Gaian perspective.

Findhorn Foundation
The Park
Forres, Moray,
Scotland IV 36 OTZ

In many ways this is the "grandmother" of new age groups, one of the first intentional spiritual communities to espouse explicitly the idea of an emerging planetary culture based on human transformation. It offers educational programs, community living, and a variety of excellent books and publications from its own press. It also offers the wisdom of its twenty-one years of experience in creating a new age community.

High Wind Association
2602 E. Newberry Boulevard
Milwaukee, WI 53211

High Wind Association is a new group that offers excellent educational programs in conjunction with the University of Wisconsin. Its most visible programs are taking shape on a farm north of Milwaukee, where the growing High Wind community has built a "bioshelter" based on design concepts developed by the New Alchemy Institute and is also designing and developing an eco-village.

Interface Foundation
230 Central Street
Newton, MA 02166

Interface is a public education organization in the Boston area offering an outstanding program of lectures, workshops, seminars—even an accredited master's degree program. At one time or another, nearly all of the leaders, visionaries, teachers, scientists, doctors, educators, writers, and poets connected with the ideas of emergence have lectured at Interface, and it is an excellent contact point for people beginning their exploration of these ideas.

Lindisfarne Association
c/o Lindisfarne Press
R.R. #2
West Stockbridge, MA 01266

An educational association exploring the synthesis of science, spirituality, literature, architecture, economics and governance in the emergence of a "meta-industrial" culture. The tapes and publications of this association are excellent, providing unique insights into the evolution of human culture.

Lorian Association
568 Grand Canyon Drive
Madison, WI 53719

This is the group with which I am most associated. Like most of the other groups listed here, we provide both long- and short-term educational programs as well as seminars conducted in various parts of the country. We have our own press, which publishes books by myself and other authors as well as a journal and other items. We also produce lecture tapes and in addition, tapes and records of music that my colleague and friend Milenko Matanovic and I, along with others, have composed. One of our principal strategies is to join with other groups, particularly the ones on this list, to coproduce joint educational and publishing ventures in order to offer the public a wide spectrum of insights and visions concerning an emerging new culture. For example, we do a regular yearly residential program with High Wind and Chinook, as well as participating in Interface and Lindisfarne programs.

Sirius Community
P.O. Box 388
Amherst, MA 01002

A spiritual community founded by and to some extent modeled after former members of Findhorn. This community offers a variety of educational programs and also acts

as a coordinator of various cooperative efforts between new
age groups throughout New England. One of the strong
points of this community is its networking with many other
groups around the world.

Windstar Foundation: Educational, Research, and Retreat
    Center
P.O. Box 286
Snowmass, CO 81654
The name of this group describes its purposes, but its
primary thrusts are in appropriate technology and as a resource center for other groups. Located not far from Aspen,
Colorado, this group was founded by a group of talented
associates of John Denver with his backing. They have
wisely not traded on his celebrity, however, but have established Windstar as a solid educational foundation, particularly in areas of environmental concern, creating a center that ably reflects the singer's values as well as their own.

BOOKS

These books represent the barest tip of the iceberg of
literature on personal and social transformation. Each read-
er's interest must guide him or her further into what is
available.

Earth at Omega. Donald Keys. New York: Branden Press,
    1982.
Global Brain, The. Peter Russell. Los Angeles: J. P.
    Tarcher, 1983.
Heart of Philosophy, The. Jacob Needleman. New York:
    Knopf, 1983.
Incomplete Guide to the Future, An. Willis Harmon. New
    York: Norton, 1979.
Little Green Book, The. John Lobell. Boulder, CO: Sham-
    bhala Press, 1981.

Millennium. Ed. by Alberto Villoldo and Ken Dychtwald.
Los Angeles: J. P. Tarcher, 1981.
Networking. Jessica Lipnack and Jeffrey Stamps. New
York: Doubleday, 1982.
Passages About Earth. William Irwin Thompson. New
York: Harper & Row, 1973.
Resettling America. Ed. by Gary Coates. Andover, MA:
Brick House, 1981.
Sane Alternative, The. James Robertson. Nashville: River
Basin, 1979.
Tomorrow Is Our Permanent Address. John and Nancy
Todd. New York: Harper & Row, 1980.

I have already mentioned throughout the text other
books that I have found useful. For those interested in my
own writings, the Lorian Association is the best place to
inquire.

PUBLICATIONS

There are a number of publications that deal with the
themes of this book, either philosophically or practically or
both. I list a few of the ones with which I am most familiar,
along with a contact address if necessary. Again, as above,
the list is very far from being complete.

Brain Mind Bulletin, Interface Press, P.O. Box 42211, 4717
N. Figueroa St., Los Angeles, CA 90042.
In Context: A Quarterly of Humane Sustainable Culture,
P.O. Box 30782, Seattle, WA 98103.
Leading Edge Bulletin, Interface Press, P.O. Box 42247,
4717 N. Figueroa St., Los Angeles, CA 90042.
Lorian Journal, Lorian Association (see above).
New Age Magazine, P.O. Box 1200, Allston, MA 02134.
One Earth, Findhorn Foundation (see above).
ReVISION, P.O. Box 316, Cambridge, MA 02138.

Index

Lindisfarne Association, 4–5,
81, 118, 134
Lindisfarne Fellows, 4–5, 51,
118–19
Lipnack, Jessica, 90, 108
Little Green Book, The, 90
Lobell, John, 90
Lorian Association, 35, 36, 52,
67, 81, 117, 120, 123, 127,
132, 134
Lovelock, James, 44, 123, 152
Lucis Trust, 19

M

Maclean, Dorothy, 33, 75
Manchester, Julia, 35
Margulis, Lynn, 103, 123, 131
Matanovic, Milenko, 52, 53,
140
Mayan, 19
Megatrends, 108
Mendlovitz, Saul, 5
Messiah, 19
Millennium, 19
Missa Gaia, 43, 44, 78, 116,
119
Morocco, 16
Morton, James Parks, 51, 124
Mumford, Lewis, 15–16, 24,
39, 64
Murphy, Michael, 140

N

Naisbitt, John, 108
Networking, 90, 108, 120
new age, 13, 17–19, 23, 27,
31–32, 34, 35–36, 38, 42,
52, 54, 59, 65, 69, 71, 75–
76, 77–84, 85, 89, 97, 98,
107, 109, 116, 117, 119,
120, 121, 136, 140, 154,
158, 161–62
new age center, 115
new age groups, 94, 126, 132
new age communities, 129–
30, 133
New Age magazine, 78, 140
new age movement, 27
new age subculture, 26
New Alchemy Institute, 5, 47,
52, 111, 116–17, 123
new paradigm, 130
New Science of Life, A, 103
New Times Network, The,
126
New World Alliance, 123
Nisbet, Robert, 11
Nostradamus, 18

O

Ogilvy, James, 73